ON FREEDOM ROAD

ON
FREEDOM
ROAD

BICYCLE EXPLORATIONS AND RECKONINGS
ON THE UNDERGROUND RAILROAD

DAVID GOODRICH

PEGASUS BOOKS
NEW YORK LONDON

ON FREEDOM ROAD

Pegasus Books, Ltd.
148 West 37th Street, 13th Floor
New York, NY 10018

Copyright © 2023 by David Goodrich

First Pegasus Books edition February 2023

Interior design by Maria Fernandez

Interior maps by Lara Andrea Taber

Library of Congress Cataloging-in-Publication Data is available.

ISBN: 978-1-63936-345-2

10 9 8 7 6 5 4 3 2 1

Printed in the United States of America
Distributed by Simon & Schuster
www.pegasusbooks.com

For Concetta
Love, best friend, editor, mom, nonna

For Charlie, Mason, Lena, Evie, and Marius
May your paths in life be full of adventures

Contents

A Note on Language

The reader will note some particular word choices in this book, and here I've been much influenced by Paul Stewart and the Underground Railroad Education Center in Albany, New York.[1] It might seem curious that the word "slave" doesn't appear except in direct quotations or contemporary usage (e.g., "slave ships"). Regarding the subjects of this book, "slaves" are not who they were; slavery is something that was done to them. So they are referred to here as "the enslaved," and those who asserted property rights are referred to as "enslavers." Similarly, referring to those making a break for freedom as "fugitives" implies the legitimacy of the legal system that supported the institution of slavery; "freedom seekers" seems a better choice.

"Black" is capitalized throughout the book, while "white" is not, following the convention of the Associated Press, the *New York Times*, and various other media. The *Times* notes that "white doesn't represent a shared culture and history in the way Black does, and also has long been capitalized by hate groups."[2]

1

Benches by the Road:
The Ride, the Underground Railroad,
and a Search for Sacred Places

I was only looking for a place out of the wind. In May 2011, eleven hundred miles into a bicycle trip from the Atlantic to the Pacific, a cold, hard headwind left me tucked down on the handlebars all morning. The water tank on the horizon announced the next town on the road: Vandalia, Illinois. An "Open" sign beckoned on the side of an old church, whose basement housed the Fayette County Museum. I stepped in, peeling off layers of clothing as I began to warm up. The expansive room was a crowded collection of furniture, display cases, and artifacts. After I wandered through displays with musty smells of faded fabric and old paper, the curator offered to show me a few favorite objects. She handed me a heavy brass ring, so big that I needed two hands to hold it. On the side, engraved in elaborate script, I read:

Belle
J. W. Goslee
Anchorage, Jefferson County, Kentucky

"That's a slave collar," she said. I took in a little breath.

Correspondence with the museum curators some years later revealed questions about the authenticity of the collar. But it didn't matter for me that day. I began to think about an invisible northbound stream of people seeking freedom, and the wheels began to turn.

I recalled an earlier journey, to the other side of the Atlantic. On a visit to England seventeen years ago, my family and I traveled to the border with Wales to find Goodrich Castle, home of one of our ancestors, according to family lore. With many of the walls destroyed in a siege long ago, it was a fixer-upper, to say the least. We stayed in nearby Bristol, a historic seaport where John Cabot embarked in 1497 as the first European to reach the mainland of North America since the Vikings. Wandering into Bristol's British Empire and Commonwealth Museum, I came upon the story of another Bristol sea captain who sailed on the brig *Sarah* some three centuries later. His name was John Goodrich. In 1789, he embarked from England as a captain on the Middle Passage.

I stepped back from the exhibit for a moment. *Oh.* Bristol had been one vertex of the infamous Triangle Trade: manufactured goods to Africa; enslaved people on the Middle Passage to the Americas; sugar, cotton, tobacco, and wealth back to England. The people of Bristol are well aware of this legacy. During Black Lives Matter protests in 2020, a statue of Edward Colston, philanthropist and slave trader, was pulled down and rolled through the city streets into the harbor.

John Goodrich kept good records. The British National Archives holds his trade book, documenting how many kegs of gunpowder and yards of cloth would make up the price for one young boy.[1] Also in existence is a 1790 letter from the ship's agent, documenting the purchase of 256 people in West Africa and the delivery of 141 to Jamaica.[2]

I'm not the first nor the last to discover a monster in my family's past. But the story at the museum pointed to how we are all tied into this institution of slavery, sometimes to a degree that inspires more than a little discomfort. The history of slavery in America is a pervasive part of the history of America, and every citizen has a connection, in some way, to this legacy. John Goodrich brought enslaved people across the ocean. Perhaps then I could discover how some of their descendants later brought themselves to freedom.

There's a certain perilous lure to the Underground Railroad for white folks like me. I'd rather believe that my ancestors were busy heroically sheltering freedom seekers on the way north than captaining slave ships.* While there were indeed prominent white figures—on this bicycle ride I will follow the roads of several—the Underground Railroad was primarily an enterprise of Black people helping enslaved Black people in their clandestine bid for freedom. Despite how large it looms in our modern imaginations, it was proportionally limited in scope. The Underground Railroad helped an estimated twenty thousand on their way to freedom. Each person had a hard-fought victory. Yet by comparison, roughly *one million* Black people were carried off from the Upper South to the Deep South in the nineteenth century to provide labor for the exploding cotton industry. As Henry Louis Gates put it, the Underground Railroad was "never as large as we often imagine, but it was real."[3]

---

* Nikole Hannah-Jones, creator of *The 1619 Project*, describes the issue this way: "Even in a story about school segregation or housing segregation, or think about the way we tell Hollywood stories of racial progress, there's always good white people at the center of that story . . . It's the way that we kind of divide our country in our heads between North and South, the true heart of America is the abolitionist North and the evil or backwards part were Southern slaveholders, but that's not who America really is." Ezra Klein Show interview, https://www .nytimes.com/2021/07/30/podcasts/transcript-ezra-klein-interviews-ta-nehisi- coates-and-nikole-hannah-jones.html

The Underground Railroad had little to do with tunnels or secret compartments in old houses. It was a network, a spiderweb of routes and people and information by which freedom seekers could escape the enslavers and their agents, helped along through various safe houses. Some branches weren't even on land; the bustling port of New York offloaded many clandestine refugees. Records were by necessity rare, as the keeping of logs was hazardous. But we do know that the Underground Railroad was primarily a phenomenon of the North and Upper South.

By riding the routes of the Underground Railroad, I couldn't hope to understand what the freedom seekers endured, leaving families behind and being hunted over hundreds of miles. But I hoped that by riding along their paths, by being out in the weather—albeit in safety and with assured food and shelter—I might get closer to the people who walked these paths, and to their descendants, and perhaps find a way to tell some of their stories. Clint Smith, who wrote of landmarks central to the history of slavery in *How the Word Is Passed*, noted "The physical place, the land people come and stand upon, is an entry point to a much broader history, of which any single location is but one piece."[4] On my journeys, I found myself often in familiar places—New Orleans and New York, Buffalo and Philadelphia—but I began to see them from a dramatically different perspective, that of desperate people from many years past.

Traveling the Underground Railroad by bicycle brings a slow tempo. In many ways, the country I'd traveled a thousand times was different: closer, experienced more nearly at the pace of the freedom seekers. A journey by bicycle also brings a certain feel for the land, different from other ways of getting around. A runner will know every hill along the route. A cyclist, in turn, comes to know watersheds and drainages, and it becomes easier to see how the land shaped the people. For example, from a bike it's easy to see how the flatlands along the Ohio River held danger for people on the run, for this was the domain of the slave-hunting gangs. Shelter lay in the hills away from the river, in the remote Quaker villages and quiet, hidden safe houses. Further south, riding on the levees along the Mississippi up from New Orleans, one can feel the pulse of the great river and imagine the flatboat that brought a young Abraham Lincoln here.

I find that these places triggered memories, research, transformations. The places where people stood are gateways, silent opening doors.

Underground Railroad Bicycle Routes: Freedom Road East:
The Harriet Tubman Route (light dashed line, 943 miles, 2019);
Freedom Road West: The River Road (dotted line, 556 miles, 2017);
Blues and the Borderland (heavy dashed line, 1497 miles, 2015).

I embarked upon a series of bicycle rides across much of the eastern United States, in total just short of 3,000 miles. The ride shown in light dash above follows an eastern branch of the Underground Railroad and the road of a tiny, hardened woman prone to seizures and visions. Harriet Tubman, the most famous of the Underground Railroad conductors, was born enslaved south of Cambridge, Maryland, in 1822. She survived a head wound caused by a lead weight thrown by an enslaver and later escaped north to Philadelphia. Tubman was in her late twenties and early thirties when she repeatedly journeyed back into the land of her bondage to rescue over seventy family members and friends.

From the distance of history, we tend to think of the North as composed of the "free" states. While the institution of slavery was abolished in the North by 1846, freedom seekers and often free Black people were subject to capture by slave hunters anywhere in the country. This was especially so after the 1850 passage of the Fugitive Slave Law. The process of returning them to their enslavers was a lucrative business. While some hotbeds of abolitionist sympathy like Oberlin or Syracuse or Boston made rendition more difficult after 1850, true freedom lay only in Canada. After that year, it was no longer safe for Tubman to stay in Philadelphia or the United States generally, so she took her family through New York City and the Hudson and Mohawk Valleys of New York to cross the Niagara River into Canada. They came to rest at Salem Chapel in Ontario. In the summer of 2019, I would follow Harriet Tubman's 940-mile route from Cambridge to that tiny chapel. This is the first section, shown here as Freedom Road East.

Two other journeys preceded the Harriet Tubman ride. These other journeys are described in detail in the second section, Freedom Road West. The ride shown as a dotted line began in what was once the epicenter for the institution of slavery: New Orleans. From the Crescent City, I rode north along the Mississippi River, headed for the Mississippi Delta on Highway 61, known as the Blues Highway. This ride ended in Clarksdale, Mississippi, heart of the Delta blues.

The first and longest of the three Underground Railroad–inspired bicycle journeys is shown above as a heavy dashed line and was first laid out by the Adventure Cycling Association. From Jackson, Mississippi, I rolled north on the Natchez Trace, the ancient road of Native American civilizations, frontier armies, and chain gangs of the enslaved. I picked up the Tennessee River through its namesake state to its junction with the Ohio in Kentucky. For much of its course, the Ohio River formed the boundary between free and slave states. My route along that river, through Kentucky, Illinois, Indiana, and Ohio, wandered through the Borderland, a kind of no-man's-land in the years before the Civil War, where slave hunters roamed both banks of the river.

Breaking from the river east of Cincinnati, I rode diagonally across Ohio. For the Kentucky-Ohio part of the route, I discovered that I was following the escape to freedom of Josiah Henson, the model for Uncle Tom in *Uncle Tom's Cabin*. Henson grew up enslaved in my hometown of Rockville, Maryland. Without consciously planning it, my route north also took me through the sites of some of Ulysses Grant's defining Civil War victories—Vicksburg, Shiloh, and Fort Donelson—as well as his hometown of Georgetown, Ohio. I called a halt in North East, Pennsylvania, on Lake Erie, where a fever brought my journey to a close. The dashed line ride was 1,497 miles, an even month on the road.

In 1989, after the publication of *Beloved*, Toni Morrison wrote:

> There is no place you or I can go, to think about or not think about, to summon the presences of, or recollect the absences of slaves . . . There is no suitable memorial or plaque or wreath or wall or park or skyscraper lobby. There's no 300-foot tower. There's no small bench by the road. There is not even a tree scored, an initial that I can visit or you can visit

in Charleston or Savannah or New York or Providence, or better still, on the banks of the Mississippi.[5]

Things have changed some since those words were committed to paper. The great angular building on the Mall in Washington, the National Museum of African American History and Culture, has opened. Away from Washington, there remain scattered sacred places. At these places, on a bicycle, I listened for the echoes of people of the Underground Railroad, of those before and after, and listened to the voices from today. In the out-of-the-way markers, the faded signs on buildings, the stories from descendants, it is possible to find examples of Toni Morrison's "bench by the road," even on the banks of the Mississippi. In Louisiana, not a thousand yards from the river, lies the house from which the greatest revolt of the enslaved in American history was launched. There are others: a great church in Philadelphia; a creaky old house backing up to the New Jersey Turnpike; a quiet little chapel in Ontario; a forest in Delaware; an industrial outbuilding in Ohio.

As I rode, I found that I was accumulating stories about historical figures, some famous, some forgotten. It became less about traveling my roads and more about discovering theirs. This book and the bicycle rides on which it is based are laid out northbound, in the direction of the unseen stream: from Cambridge, Maryland, to Canada in the East and from New Orleans toward Canada in the South and Midwest. The journeys were like riding through a dark forest on a bright winter day, with the stories like sharp flashes of light coming through the trees.

To begin this great south-to-north sweep, consider the outstretched hand on a mural overlooking a parking lot in Cambridge, Maryland.

2

Freedom Road East:
The Trail of Harriet Tubman

i. The Hand Reaching Out (Maryland)

knew we were on the right road when I saw the mural. We were wandering through Cambridge, Maryland, near where Harriet Tubman had been enslaved. A handwritten sign, *Mural* →, was posted on the main street, as though local people were tired of answering the same question. She revealed herself behind the Harriet Tubman Museum and Educational Center, on the wall of a building overlooking a parking lot. She was huge, breathtaking. Harriet Tubman appeared to have broken through the bricks of the wall, beckoning the viewer to come into her world. As the mural was being completed, one of the local shop owners snapped a photo of her three-year-old Black granddaughter reaching up to touch the hand. The photo went viral.

*Harriet Tubman mural "Take My Hand" by
Michael Rosato, Cambridge, Maryland.*

Rick Sullivan, Lynn Salvo, and I were in Harriet Tubman's company in the long shadows of that late June afternoon. We three cyclists had spent the winter and spring training for this ride. Rick introduced me to the blues in the Mississippi Delta some years before and carried a folding guitar on the back of his bike; more on him in Freedom Road West. He would have to leave the ride in New York City.

Lynn is in a different place from other cyclists I know. She holds the Guinness Record for oldest woman to ride across the United States. In 2018, she also became the oldest woman to ride across Canada. Lynn is the Queen of Fifty. Rick or I might be stronger, at times, early during any given day's ride, but as shadows grow long and the mileage ticks over fifty, she moves into her domain. We spent a lot of time looking at a gray braid coming out of a cycling helmet. Well into her seventies, she's not merely a cyclist but an athlete.

The name of Lynn's brother, John West, is on the Vietnam Veterans Memorial in Washington. An F-4 Phantom pilot, he was lost over Laos in 1970. Lynn remembers John, and his loss. Our ride north together was to be a small part of the giant peace sign she was inscribing on the continent. Between Lynn and Harriet, I was destined to follow two small, strong women north to Ontario that summer. We touched the hand for luck.

My wife, Concetta, drove us around Cambridge, and she would meet us again 700 miles down the road in Central New York. Later that night, she drove us past the Dorchester County Courthouse, lit up in floodlights. Harriet Tubman's niece Kessiah and her two children had stood on the auction block there in 1850. In a carefully choreographed plan, Kessiah's free Black husband, John Bowley, outbid everyone just before lunch. When the official came to collect afterward, Bowley had spirited his wife and daughters away, sailing with his family in a log canoe across the Chesapeake Bay to Baltimore. He met Tubman there, and she brought them on safely to Philadelphia.

Harriet Tubman is the most famous and mythologized participant in the Underground Railroad. Her story is told so often in children's books that we seem to forget she was real. Basketball Hall of Famer Kareem Abdul-Jabbar tells of a teacher friend who tests students during Black History Month at a grade school outside Atlanta. "Her kids," Abdul-Jabbar writes, "know so little about Black history that they answer Harriet Tubman for everything."[1] Her face is to be on the $20 bill, and she was the subject of a 2019 movie.*

The truth is worthy of the myth. Born into slavery as Araminta Ross, she began as an enslaved domestic, then increasingly worked in the fields and woods. Among other jobs, she worked hauling logs, sometimes cutting half a cord of wood a day. Faced with the likelihood that she would be sold south like her three sisters, she made her break for

---

* Treasury Secretary Janet Yellen has indicated that the Tubman $20 is on track but won't be out before 2030.

freedom in 1849, reaching Philadelphia. Incredibly, she would return to the land of her enslavement, the Eastern Shore of Maryland, at least thirteen times, bringing at a minimum seventy people to freedom. During the Civil War, she was a scout and spy for the Union Army and led commando raids into Georgia and South Carolina.

THREE HUNDRED DOLLARS REWARD.

RANAWAY from the subscriber on Monday the 17th ult., three negroes, named as follows: HARRY, aged about 19 years, has on one side of his neck a wen, just under the ear, he is of a dark chestnut color, about 5 feet 8 or 9 inches hight; BEN, aged aged about 25 years, is very quick to speak when spoken to, he is of a chestnut color, about six feet high; MINTY, aged about 27 years, is of a chestnut color, fine looking, and about 5 feet high. One hundred dollars reward will be given for each of the above named negroes, if taken out of the State, and $50 each if taken in the State. They must be lodged in Baltimore, Easton or Cambridge Jail, in Maryland.

ELIZA ANN BRODESS,
Near Bucktown, Dorchester county, Md.
Oct. 3d, 1849.

☞The Delaware Gazette will please copy the above three weeks, and charge this office.

Harriet "Minty" Tubman's original runaway advertisement, offering a reward for her capture.

An event during her adolescence marked her entire life. At a local store, as another enslaved man was trying to avoid a beating, his overseer picked up a two-pound weight and threw it at him. He missed and hit Tubman in the head, fracturing her skull. She was near death for several days, and she took weeks to recover. For the rest of her life, she would frequently fade out of consciousness, often in midsentence. Modern speculation is that these were symptoms of temporal lobe epilepsy caused by the trauma. Yet her handicap was also her power. The injury marked the start of a lifetime of potent dreams and visions that she claimed would portend the future.[2] It also deepened an already strong faith. Her friends and family said "the whites can't catch her because you see she's born with the charm. The Lord has given Moses the power."[3]

Certainly Tubman believed that the Lord protected her, but she took great care to cover her tracks in any case. She could not read or write, and written records would have been a liability regardless. That made finding her route a challenge for me, in part because we know she took different paths depending on the intensity of patrols, availability of safe houses, and presence of guards on bridges, trains, and boats.

Tubman was by necessity a wraith. In the 1850s, she moved through a veiled domain of safe houses, swamps, graveyards, and night travel, a secret world parallel to that of white people. In the movie *Harriet*, she is often portrayed as running. Harriet would never run. She would not want to attract attention. Anonymity was her shield. She wanted to melt into the landscape, to appear frail, even to pose as an old woman. The enslavers of the Eastern Shore knew that something was going on; they were losing too much of what they considered to be their property. They were sure that it had to be the work of Northern white abolitionists. It never occurred to them that a small Black woman could cause them so much trouble.

I wanted to get closer to the myth by following her route north to freedom. But how to find the tracks of a phantom? In Maryland and Delaware, it was quite easy. Tubman's route through these two states is superbly mapped and described on the Harriet Tubman Underground Railroad Byway site, run by the states of Maryland and Delaware. The online map extends from Cambridge to Philadelphia, exploring existing Underground Railroad sites and stopping places along the way. Tubman's passage to Philadelphia usually ended at the residence of William Still, a free African American and leader of the Anti-Slavery Office there.

But in 1850, with the passage of the Fugitive Slave Law, Tubman realized that Philadelphia, and indeed the entire United States, was not safe for formerly enslaved people seeking to remain free. There would be no sanctuary cities. The arc of the moral universe was not bending toward justice. Moses must lead her people to a new Promised Land, 850 miles away: St. Catharines, Ontario.

While her route through Maryland and Delaware is well documented, my task before embarking on the trip was to find her route from Philadelphia to St. Catharines. It wasn't as easy as it might seem. For someone as well known as Harriet Tubman, the Web, that font of all knowledge, had surprisingly little. So I was forced to make a pilgrimage to one of my favorite places: the Reading Room of the Library of Congress. It's one of the most magnificent spaces in Washington, yet few people see it. I sat at an old wooden desk waiting for books with a few other researchers, looking up at a resplendent golden rotunda, surrounded by statues of scientists and musicians, philosophers and explorers. The musty, comforting smell of the stacks wafts through. Surely one could learn anything here.

It was only late in the day that I began to come across what I needed. A twenty-five-year-old guide to the Underground Railroad by historian Charles Blockson had, as an appendix, a driving tour following Tubman's route.[4] Blockson would later donate a collection of Tubman artifacts, including her hymnal, to the National Museum of African

American History and Culture. I also found Kate Clifford Larson's seminal Tubman biography, *Bound for the Promised Land*, detailed and well researched.

The references showed many routes, varying according to availability of safe houses ("stations") and activity of slave hunters. The most direct way to Canada from Philadelphia lay across central Pennsylvania to the Finger Lakes of New York. A relatively small number of freedom seekers traveled this way, but they faced a journey through a remote, rugged region. The area is known as the Endless Mountains. I've ridden through it by bike, and I can affirm that it comes by the name honestly.

Route of the Harriet Tubman Ride, 2019. Cambridge, Maryland to St. Catharines, Ontario (dashed).

So the path of our ride would be an amalgam. It would begin in the land of Tubman's enslavement, the Eastern Shore of Maryland, then through Delaware to Philadelphia. From there, the route makes a great bend north to New York City, up the Hudson Valley to Albany, then west across the Mohawk Valley and Erie Canal to Buffalo. Freedom seekers would finally cross the Niagara River to reach Salem Chapel in St. Catharines, Ontario, where the Tubman family came to live and give thanks. This route, while less direct than the path through central Pennsylvania, had the advantage of providing multiple options for the journey, including by water. Many traveled at least in part by ship on the Chesapeake Bay, Delaware River, Atlantic Ocean, or Hudson River. The eastern route also offered shelter in the well-established abolitionist communities of Philadelphia, New York, Albany, and Syracuse.

We rolled our bikes out of the Cambridge motel lobby. We would follow this quietest of our national heroes as she wound her way on a path that tracks through the middle of today's megalopolis. We would slip through the underside of great cities, close to the land and out in the weather as Tubman and her charges had been. For us, the path would include concrete tunnels below thundering interstates, forest trails into metropolises, and a ferry ride past the Statue of Liberty, built during her lifetime. We turned out onto the open road, following the mural's outstretched hand.

ii. Flight of the Brothers (Maryland)

We left the motel on a blustery, clear day and rode out into the flatlands of Maryland's Eastern Shore. My two sturdy friends joined me for the ride north. Before his retirement, Rick had commuted by bike through the winter. He'd ridden with me across Louisiana, Mississippi, and

Tennessee, sharing the experiences that make up many of the later chapters of this book. For Lynn, this ride was just a small section of the 6,500 miles that she would log toward her transcontinental peace sign that year. She and I had joined in a well-choreographed ride across the Canadian prairie starting in Moose Jaw, Saskatchewan, the year before. The Harriet Tubman ride would be the first time that Lynn, Rick, and I would ride together. At 12 miles per hour, the three of us flew across the land compared to the cautious foot travelers of the Underground Railroad.

From right: Lynn Salvo, Rick Sullivan, and the author, northbound.

The area was filled with stories. For the Maryland section of the ride, the Harriet Tubman Underground Railroad Byway app provided a narrative at each of the sites we'd visit. We seemed to be flashing between the pleasures and trials of a long bike tour and harrowing tales of nineteenth-century slavery.

Our first day was a 50-mile circuit starting in Cambridge, a day trip south before turning north to Canada. This loop was both a shakedown ride and a visit to Tubman's home. We wanted Concetta to follow us in the car that day, for if something were to go wrong, we'd probably know it early. After Cambridge, we three riders would be on our own for the next 300 miles.

We rode straight into the teeth of a headwind coming off the Chesapeake Bay. As we were passing the last convenience store we'd see that day, the cardboard carton of a twelve-pack, hurled by the wind, bounced across the road. Lynn narrowly missed hitting it.

This was the land of Harriet Tubman's family and of her youth, and much of her story is rooted in this place. Despite the horrors of her enslavement, the Eastern Shore was where her family lived, and where she would return again and again. In 2021, archaeologists discovered the site of the cabin where she and her family lived.[5] Now as then, it's rural, a land of farms and forests and marshes along the Chesapeake Bay, not built up or paved like the great cities we would be visiting later. Arguably, the region was even more developed back in the 1840s, with bustling ports a contrast to the small marinas on the water in the present day. Today the biggest threat is the water itself. Climate change has arrived here, like everywhere. The land is low and the water is rising.

In the early 1800s, this area south of Cambridge was a training ground for Harriet Tubman, building the strength and knowledge for a future she could not yet imagine. We rode through the forests where Tubman had been hired out to work on her father's lumber crew. Though barely five feet tall, she was prodigiously strong. She hauled logs, and reportedly her master often exhibited her feats of strength to his friends.[6] Lumber camp required being comfortable in the woods, a skill that would come in handy later. Baltimore shipbuilders prized the timber she cut. The trees that Tubman felled provided ribs for wooden ships that sailed the world, among them the famed Baltimore clippers.

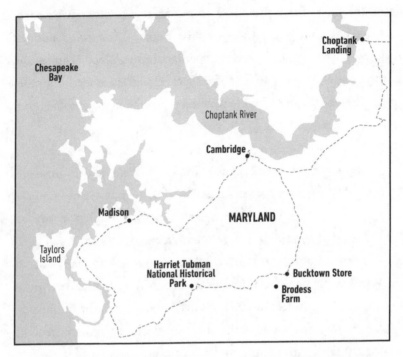

Start of the ride: Harriet Tubman country and bike route, Maryland Eastern Shore. The first day's ride started and ended in Cambridge.

We approached Madison, a town sitting on an arm of the Chesapeake. We paused to drink and to look out on the water. The marina was filled with watermen's boats known as deadrises, workboats with a small cabin forward and a large work area aft for handling crab pots. Out on the bay, white sailboats took advantage of the stiff breeze. I'd been out there on a research ship thirty-six years before, another white ship on the horizon. Back then we dodged those sailboats and put out instruments to measure the currents. I know this water well.

Harriet Tubman was born near Madison and later loaded timber onto ships in this port, which was then much larger and known as Tobacco Stick. Free Black sailors would pass through from up and down the East Coast, providing an informal and vital news network that extended far beyond the Eastern Shore. They gave Tubman a window on the world. On the next peninsula north, not 12 miles away as the crow flies, the enslaved Frederick Douglass looked out on the same Chesapeake in 1834. He recalled that time in his autobiography, written a decade later:

> Those beautiful vessels, robed in purest white, so delightful to the eye of freemen, were to me so many shrouded ghosts, to terrify and torment me with thoughts of my wretched condition. I have often, in the deep stillness of a summer's Sabbath, stood all alone upon the lofty banks of that noble bay, and traced with saddened heart and tearful eye, the countless number of sails moving off to the mighty ocean. . . You are loosed from your moorings and are free; I am fast in my chains, and am a slave. . . Alas betwixt me and you, the turbid waters roll.[7]

Douglass would shadow us on this journey, for he traveled along many of the same roads as Tubman. Douglass was a natural writer and a soaring orator, while Tubman, though illiterate, possessed a boundless physical and emotional strength. We would cross Douglass's path again in Manhattan, and once more in Central New York, where he and Tubman are buried a day's bike ride apart.

Not far from Madison is where a free Black man named Jacob Jackson once lived, a place that was the origin of one of Harriet Tubman's most famous escapes. The year was 1854, long after her own escape. Tubman had been in Ontario for some time, her legend beginning to grow. By word of mouth and overheard conversations, Jackson found out that Harriet's three brothers—Ben, Robert, and Henry—were to be sold, and he wrote Harriet. She had already lost her three sisters to slave traders. Dictating a letter to a friend, she wrote Jackson back, "Tell my brothers to be always watching unto prayer, and when the good old ship of Zion comes along, be ready to step aboard." The letter was intercepted by postal inspectors, and Jackson was questioned. They showed him the letter, and he professed ignorance. But the message he passed on to her brothers was clear: Be prepared to run.

We passed in sight of a place called Buttons Creek. Jane Kane, fiancée to Harriet's brother Ben, was enslaved there by a particularly brutal man. In a later interview, she describes having been beaten "until the blood ran from my nose and my mouth" and being locked in a cupboard until she nearly suffocated. Her enslaver would not allow her to marry Ben, so one night Ben hid a set of men's clothing in the garden. On Christmas Eve 1854, in a plot twist worthy of Shakespeare, Jane slipped out disguised as a man.[8] She headed north, bound for Ben and freedom.

We rode past the site of Brodess Farm, where Tubman and her family were enslaved. In 1849, at age twenty-seven, on hearing rumors that she might be sold, she slipped away from the Brodesses and reached the relative safety of Philadelphia. Five years later, Ben, Robert, and Henry waited there, knowing that they would be auctioned off the day after Christmas. But they had a legal reason to be on the road. The enslaved were often allowed to visit family over the holiday. Their parents, Ben Sr. and Rit, lived north of Cambridge at a place called Poplar Neck. The good ship of Zion would leave from there. The brothers were on the move. Jane Kane was making the 40-mile trip as well.

On Christmas Day 1854, Tubman waited in a corn crib not far from her parents' cabin with Ben, Henry, Jane, and two others, waiting for their chance to run that night. Robert wasn't there and, according to her rules, Tubman "never waited for no one." Robert had a good reason for being late. His wife Mary was in labor, and she would give birth to their third child that night. Robert had an impossible choice. If he stayed, he would be on the auction block in two days. If he left, he might never see his family again.

One family was reunited that night: Ben and Jane would make it all the way to Ontario together. Another was broken: Robert would hurry to catch up to his brothers, leaving his family behind, including the newborn baby girl, Harriet. Mary, who could not escape, would remarry, and she would be freed in 1862. Robert would later come back to Cambridge, after the Civil War, for his two sons.

On that Christmas Day, no one told Harriet's mother, Rit, that her children were nearby. Tubman later passed on to her biographer that Rit might "cause such an uproar in her efforts to retain them that the whole plantation would have been alarmed."[9] Rit's daughter and sons watched her cook dinner through the slats of the corn crib. She waited for her family that night, yet they never arrived. But ultimately Harriet Tubman would return for both of her parents.

Harriet and her party slipped away on Christmas night into a cold world filled with slave patrols. Ben Sr., Harriet's father, would follow his children blindfolded through the woods as they started on their flight, turning back before too long. He could later tell the slave hunters honestly that he hadn't seen them. Avoiding main roads, Harriet guided her family through the woods in the darkness, through brambles, swamps, and stream crossings. She had come to prefer the long winter nights for her escapes, as the longer-lasting darkness provided cover for greater distances. They would hide at safe houses by day, often with free Black people (like her parents, who often hid freedom seekers) or Quakers. It's some measure of their trial that Harriet and one of the men needed new shoes by the time they reached Wilmington. When they arrived at the office of

Philadelphia conductor William Still, the brothers celebrated their freedom by taking new names.

On bicycles, our route from the port of Madison passed through the forest and out onto a marsh. We paused on a bridge over a little stream. Something was odd about the stream. It was perfectly straight, not meandering at all. We were passing over Stewarts Canal, a water passage that connected the bay with the productive forests and fields of the interior. It was dug over twenty years, in the early 1800s, primarily by enslaved Black people in the heat of the mosquito-infested swamps.

This part of the world is thin on lunch establishments. In fact, it boasts only one: Palm Beach Willie's, a floating dock bar and grill at Taylors Island. Heavy fried seafood might not sit well for the afternoon's ride, but no matter: Lynn had arranged for her family to meet us there, so, with Concetta, we had our own little midday party.

When our leaden legs slowly got to turning again after lunch, we were, fortunately, on the downwind reach. We were tucked into the wind, at the point where the tailwind matched our speed. In our calm shell, pedaling was effortless, while to either side the grass blew in the wind. While we rode encased in a wind cocoon, the cry of ospreys provided the background music.

Across the Blackwater Bridge lay the Visitor Center to the Harriet Tubman Underground Railroad National Historical Park, dedicated and officially opened in 2017. It's laid out with care and attention to detail. Tubman's bust is at exactly her height. The building is oriented to the north. In the exhibits is a schematic map of Tubman's route that I'd seen on a first visit the year before. I remember looking at that map and thinking, *I can ride this*. The seed was planted. On the entrance video, we saw interviews with people who run historical sites, people whom we would meet up the road. We learned that there is a modern Underground Railroad history network that extends clear to Canada.

After the Visitor Center, the road curved toward the Blackwater National Wildlife Refuge. Concetta is a birder, and for her it's a quiet wonderland, with 295 species of birds and one of the largest populations of bald eagles on the East Coast. Red-tailed hawks perch on dead limbs. Egrets and herons pace the marshes. Back in the woods, nuthatches and indigo buntings flit between the trees. Just offshore was where I glimpsed my first image of the Chesapeake, back in seafaring days. We were on a small boat lost in the fog. Emerging from the mist was a waterman on the stern of a deadrise, pulling up a set of long scissor-like oyster tongs.

The Blackwater is beautiful but eerie, with the footprints of climate change much in evidence. Amid the sounds of ospreys overhead, we passed panoramas of dead trees. Since it's so flat, the land is quite susceptible to sea level rise. Ghost forests, where trees have been killed by saltwater intrusion, litter the Refuge. Between 1938 and 2006, 3,000 acres of forest and agricultural land have become marsh. And more than 5,000 acres of marsh became open water.[10] Today the Blackwater is drowning. It isn't the only place in Tubman country threatened by the advancing sea. Malone's Methodist Episcopal Church, the first African American church established on the Eastern Shore after the Civil War and a stop on the Tubman Byway, frequently finds water underfoot even on sunny days.[11]

For the child Harriet Tubman, this was a harsh place. Late fall to early winter was the time for trapping muskrats, when their fur was at its fullest. At six years old, the Brodesses hired her out to wade through the frozen marshes, checking on traps. Consider stepping into the Blackwater in December, wind whipping through the marsh grass, a skin of ice along the shoreline. After her wades, she frequently fell ill and was sent back to the farm. Early on, she learned brutal lessons in endurance, survival, and invisibility, lessons she would put to good use.

We finished the easy ride back to Cambridge with all our gear in working order. Our one-day, 50-mile shakedown ride was over, and we would have no car trailing us until we passed New York City. Turning north, we would be on our own, embarking on the same 900-mile journey as Tubman's family, except that we would be traveling by daylight, without dogs in pursuit, and with the benefit of Gore-Tex, shiny gears, and freedom.

The next day, about 14 miles up the road, we took a lunch break at a place called Choptank Landing. It was a crisp, perfect day, the wind blowing whitecaps across the wide Choptank River. The cool water felt perfect on our feet as we waded out into the water. A few hundred yards up the river lay Poplar Neck, where Ben and Rit's corncrib once sat.

Tubman and her brothers were northbound. In very different circumstances, 155 years later, we were, too.

iii. Thunder on the Hill (Delaware)

I couldn't get in touch. The recording said, "Have a blessed day," and messages left on the voicemail and on the Facebook page brought no reply. But we had one more shot. It happened that we would be riding through on a Sunday morning. Maybe we would just stop in for services. We had to try. After all, this was the Star of the East.

The Star Hill African Methodist Episcopal (AME) Church in Dover, Delaware, has a long history with the Underground Railroad. There aren't many hills in Delaware. Star Hill was built on a little rise by a local Black congregation in 1842 so that freedom seekers might be able to see it. The local historian speculated that the congregation originally called it Star of the East because freedom seekers would actually be coming east from Maryland. As we would discover on our way to Canada, the AME churches were central stops on the road to freedom. This one still stands. We wanted to see it, at least from the outside.

The early morning sun was firing up for a hot one. We had a 60-mile day laid out, starting north on the Eastern Shore through Greensboro, Maryland, then to Sandtown, Dover, and Wilmington, Delaware. In interviews long after her Underground Railroad days, Harriet Tubman told historian Wilbur Siebert that this was her preferred route. As we rolled north into the heat, we made a first stop before crossing into Delaware.

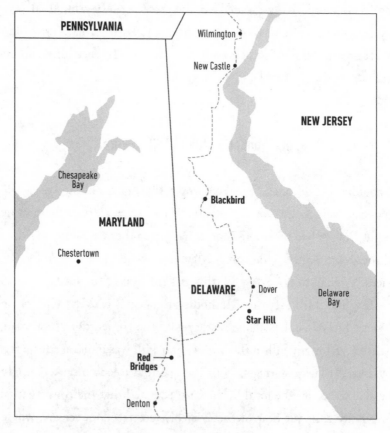

Bicycle route through Delaware.

Almost immediately after turning off the main road north of Denton, we began to regret it. The road turned to loose dirt and gravel. On the downhill stretch, I began to fishtail, almost going down several times. Up ahead, Lynn was having a hard time finding a line through the soft sand. Then the grade gradually settled out into a deep, cool forest. After dismounting from the bikes, we wandered into a quiet little wonderland by the river. The stream gently coursed over a small dam, and we dangled our feet in the water.

The spot is known as Red Bridges, and it's the first place where the Choptank River is narrow and shallow enough to wade across. Freedom seekers would cross here, far back in the woods, to a place just a few miles from the state line. More patrols and hunters waited once they crossed into Delaware, but the travelers were almost out of Maryland. There was a feeling of sacredness to this little glen. Sunbeams filtered down through the trees, and the sound of moving water was in the background. On the opposite bank, a dad was teaching his daughter how to fish. On his phone, Rick found a version of the spiritual "Wade in the Water." We know that Harriet Tubman used songs as signals when leading groups on the run, and this may have been one of the songs. The lines filtered out through the glen:

> *Who's that young girl dressed in red?*
> *Must be the children that Moses led.*
> *Who's that young girl dressed in white?*
> *Must be the children of the Israelite.*
> *Who's that yonder dressed in blue?*
> *Must be the children that made it through.*
> *God gonna trouble the water . . .*

The cool woods were tempting, but Sunday prayers waited. We rolled back out onto the main road. Lynn pulled us over for a quick selfie at the Delaware sign, the first state line we would cross. Through the hazy soybean fields, the only breeze was the one we generated. Two hours and twenty miles later, covered in sweat, we rode up to a little red-roofed chapel. The sound of clapping hands and a gospel hymn told of the services going on inside. A woman appeared at the door, eyeing us warily. With their history of being targeted and terrorized, I suspect that Black churches have a certain radar for strangers. We explained about the Tubman ride and asked if we might sit in. She nodded and motioned with her hand.

We eased into the back pew of the tiny blue-walled chapel, trying unsuccessfully to be discreet. The parishioners, in Sunday best, occasionally glanced back at the odd group in spandex behind them. A simple wooden cross hung over the altar. The congregation was primarily African American women, the occasional wave of a fan in evidence. During the hymns, the congregation swayed in the heat, hands reaching above white dresses. John Jordan, the minister, delivered a thunderous sermon in an emotional call-and-response style. His stories of sin and redemption went from biblical allegories to tales of the everyday. Salvation rolled down like water. In the midst of the sermon, two women in lace church hats and white gloves slipped out of the chapel. A few moments later they reappeared with our own salvation, a glass of ice water for each of us. The minister continued:

> Y'all know I always like to stop for coffee in the morning at the Wawa. Now there's usually a couple of people in line behind me. And sometimes I'll tell the clerk to ring up all of their orders, too. Then I'll walk out, but I can't look at their faces. Because it's not about me, and it's not about them. It's to the greater glory of the Lord.

It was Father's Day. He recognized the fathers and, to numerous amens, "the women who became fathers." As the service closed, the ushers passed out envelopes wrapped in gold braid with a handwritten "Happy Father's Day" inscription. Inside was a small brownie and a sheet of prayers. Among them was Matthew 11:28-30: "Come to me, all you who are weary and heavy laden with care. I will give you rest."

After the service, the parishioners fussed over us. The ladies in white gloves, Sondra Ross and Hattie Hogan, led us over to the adjacent hall for refreshments.

"You have to meet Lucreatia," they said. "She's who you want to talk to." Lucreatia Wilson is the local historian and a longtime member of the church. She pointed to where, under the old chapel, "we sheltered the runaways." Some years back, she sponsored a panel of Tubman's great-nieces at Star Hill.

"Do you think that Harriet Tubman came through here?" I asked.

"She had to come this way," Lucreatia said. "These were Quaker farms, not like [nearby] Camden. The Quakers donated the land for the church, and some of them helped the runaways. We know that she stayed with several conductors around here, like William and Nathaniel Brinkley and Abraham Gibbs. This was the route around Camden."

"You seem to know everything about Star Hill."

"Well, I've been involved with the church since 1952. Before then, we lived in San Antonio, in the Jim Crow South. I still remember the white line on the bus that we had to sit behind. Then my father was stationed at Dover Air Force Base, so we moved up here.

"When I was growing up, we knew a farmer and a minister by the name of Solomon Gibbs. Several times a week he would gather us at the vegetable garden and tell us stories of slavery and the Underground

Railroad. I was just a kid, and I didn't pay him much attention. But God had a plan. It didn't come until later when I was driving home from taking my daughter to college. The voice came and said, 'You will teach history. You will tell the story.'"

"So now I do tours around the area of the Underground Railroad sites. And I used to have kids into the church to talk about what the people went through. We'd cut muslin, potato sack material, into squares, then put jerky, raisins, peanuts on it. Then we'd tie the muslin onto a stick and take the kids on a hike down by the stream to give them an idea of what it was like."

"It must be quite something to live just down the road from this little church," I said.

"I love this church more than I love my home," she said.

We left Lucreatia and the congregation and headed north toward the main stretch of Dover. Dover has a special place in the lore of the Underground Railroad. In 1857, eight of the enslaved escaped from Bucktown, where Tubman had left eight years before.[12] She gave them instructions for the way north, including stopping by the home of one Black conductor, Thomas Otwell, in Delaware. But Otwell had succumbed to the temptation of the $3000 reward for the eight, an enormous amount of money at the time. He led them to the second floor of the Dover jail, where they were to be held that night, ostensibly for their protection. As the freedom seekers became suspicious, the sheriff appeared and went to his living quarters to get a gun. They followed him. One grabbed a shovel full of embers from the fireplace and threw them across the room, while the others escaped out a window. The sheriff's gun misfired as the last one made his break. All eight would eventually make it to Canada and one, Thomas Elliott, became Tubman's right-hand man in Ontario. In newspapers from Ontario to Delaware, they would become known as the Dover Eight.[13]

Though Tubman must have rejoiced at the escape, the publicity and the resulting reaction from the enslavers of the Eastern Shore made life especially hard for Underground Railroad conductors. Her father, Ben Ross, who was free, was rightly suspected to be one. He and her mother, Rit, had indeed sheltered the eight on their way north. Now the heat was coming, and they likely knew that their situation was precarious. That year, one prominent free Black conductor, Rev. Samuel Green, was arrested and sentenced to ten years for the crime of having abolitionist literature, namely *Uncle Tom's Cabin*, in his possession.

It was time for Harriet to come back for her parents, now in their seventies. They must have dreaded the prospect of the 800-mile journey ahead. Harriet slipped south by her usual clandestine routes. At her parents' house on Poplar Neck, she rigged a curious contraption. As their conductor in Delaware described it, "They started with an old horse, fitted out in primitive style with a straw collar, a pair of old chaise wheels, with a board on the axle to sit on, another board swung with ropes, fastened to the axle, to rest their feet on."[14] Ben brought his broadaxe and Rit her featherbed tick, a cotton bag filled with feathers, and they started north. They passed through Philadelphia, New York, and Rochester on their way to the Promised Land in St. Catharines.[15]

Our road north this day was busier and faster than it had been in the nineteenth century, with semis rumbling by and heat shimmering off the four-lane US 13, once known as the Kings Highway. The blessedly wide shoulder kept the trucks a few feet away, but we were blowing through our water bottles at an impressive pace. We turned off US 13 as soon as we could, bound for a place that Tubman knew well.

She noted in interviews after the Civil War that a place called "Blackbird" was one of her landmarks as she journeyed through Delaware. In her day there were one or more free Black settlements here, far from the major towns. Today it lends its name to a state forest where asphalt and strip malls give way first to farms, then deep woods. Blackbird was a place to hide by day, travel by night. By the roadside, Lynn found leaves of the sweet gum tree and their seedpods, covered with burrs. As Kate Clifford Larson describes in her Tubman biography, these cover the forest floor, a bed of nails for those freedom seekers on the run without shoes. She also describes how Tubman, beset with a toothache near Blackbird, dispensed with the offending tooth with a rock.[16]

The story of the Underground Railroad in Delaware and Pennsylvania is very much intertwined with the Quakers. Given the nature of her work, Tubman didn't leave business cards, but she almost certainly visited the Appoquinimink Friends Meeting House in Odessa. It's still there, behind an old brick wall, a small building with spartan wood benches, surrounded by graveyards dating to the birth of the nation. Next to one gravestone is a steel star with the initials "G.A.R," for Grand Army of the Republic. This man fought for the Union. The Quakers made room for soldiers.

One particular Quaker was intimately tied to the Underground Railroad in Delaware. Thomas Garrett ran an iron, coal, and hardware business in Wilmington and kept meticulous notes of the freedom seekers he aided over the course of three decades.[17] He claimed to have helped over 2,200 by the time of the Civil War. He would come to know Tubman well. As she passed through his home repeatedly, his respect for her only grew. He wrote that he was amazed that Tubman "does not know, or appears not to know, that she has done anything worth notice."[18] Garrett used her dramatic stories to raise money from abolitionist supporters, some as far away as England, and she called on him for help many times. He recounted in one of his letters:

On one occasion when I had not seen her for three months, she came into my store. I said, "Harriet, I am glad to see thee! I suppose thee wants a pair of new shoes." Her reply was "I want more than that." I, in jest, said, "I have always been liberal with thee, and wish to be; but I am not rich, and cannot afford to give much." Her reply was: "God tells me you have money for me." I asked her "if God never deceived her?" She said, "No!" "Well! how much does thee want?" After studying a moment, she said: "About twenty-three dollars." I then gave her twenty-four.[19]

We found the place where Garrett's activities had run him afoul of the law, well before meeting Tubman. New Castle was the first capital of Delaware, and its stately red brick courthouse still stands. Garrett was tried here in 1848, the year before Tubman's flight, for helping a Black family of eight escape. Presiding over the trial was US Supreme Court chief justice Roger Taney. If ever there were a hanging judge for the Underground Railroad, that would be Taney. Nine years later, he would author the infamous Dred Scott decision, holding that Black people could never be US citizens and unraveling the delicate string of compromises over the institution of slavery that had held the Union together. At New Castle, Taney's fine essentially bankrupted Garrett. After the verdict, the defendant turned to the spectators and declared, "If any of you know of any slave who needs assistance, send him to me."

As we rode north from New Castle to Wilmington, we faced an obstacle unknown to the freedom seekers of the nineteenth century: the main artery of the East Coast megalopolis, I-295, the interstate leading to the Delaware Memorial Bridge. I've driven my car over this stretch hundreds of times, with its eight lanes of asphalt and not an overpass in sight. As we approached this massive wall of concrete by bicycle, I began to wonder how we could possibly cross. Would we be lugging loaded bikes over guardrails and scampering across traffic? Yet nothing we'd read about the bike route indicated a problem. As we came upon the interstate, a little tunnel came into view, and we rode through to the continuing rumble of traffic overhead. The next stretch was a delight. The Jack Markell Trail crosses the Christina River before becoming a boardwalk across a marsh and wildlife refuge. It deposited us on the Riverwalk in downtown Wilmington.

Frederick Douglass wrote of being on the run, "At every gate through which we were to pass, we saw a watchman—at every ferry a guard—on every bridge a sentinel—and in every wood a patrol."[20] One such place was the Market Street Bridge in Wilmington. In November of 1856, Tubman accompanied a group of four north from the Choptank River country. Slave hunters hotly pursued them. One of the four, Josiah "Joe" Bailey, had a $1500 price on his head. We'd encounter him again later in our journey, on the bridge to Canada. Tubman and her party approached Wilmington after a roundabout two-week journey up the Eastern Shore, but they stopped on the far side of the Christina River. Police patrolled the Market Street Bridge, and posters for their capture were everywhere.

Tubman sent word ahead, by messenger, to Garrett across the river in Wilmington. Garrett made a plan. He dispatched two wagons filled with bricks across the bridge. The wagons returned that evening, without attracting suspicion from the guards. Inside the brick piles were the freedom seekers.[21]

Statue of Harriet Tubman and Thomas Garrett,
Tubman–Garrett Park, Wilmington.

Today, next to the Market Street Bridge, is a city park graced by a dramatic statue of Tubman and Garrett. We stretched our legs on the benches. Garrett embraced his role as the lead conductor in Wilmington for the Underground Railroad. He would pass freedom seekers on to the Quakers of Kennett Square in Pennsylvania and to the famed Black conductor of Philadelphia, William Still. After mass escapes of the enslaved in late 1857, referred to in the newspapers of the time as the "Slave Stampede," it became too dangerous for Tubman to return to the Eastern Shore. She spent several years in the North, caring for her parents, raising money, and speaking to abolitionist audiences. But in December 1860, William Still opened a letter from Thomas Garrett. A line from that letter is engraved on the marker in the Wilmington park: "I write to let thee know that Harriet Tubman is again in these parts."

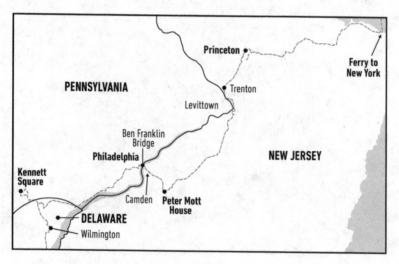

Bicycle route through Pennsylvania and New Jersey, from Wilmington, Delaware, to the Seastreak Ferry at Highlands, New Jersey.

iv. In the Company of Friends (Pennsylvania)

The memory of a photograph from long ago had lodged in the back of my head. Women dressed in bonnets and hoop skirts and stern bearded men in bow ties and black suits look out from the front of a massive white clapboard building. The Longwood Progressive Meetinghouse in Kennett Square was built in 1855, becoming the center for a hotbed of abolition in Pennsylvania's Brandywine Valley. By night, Harriet Tubman would climb the hills out of Wilmington with her charges, seeking out the company and the shelter of these people, before moving on to Philadelphia and William Still.

Longwood Meeting, Kennett Square, Pennsylvania, 1865. Abolitionist William Lloyd Garrison is at the right, holding a bouquet. In a top hat at the door is Wilmington conductor and Tubman friend, Thomas Garrett.

We climbed Harriet's steep hills behind Wilmington to Kennett Square, crossing the border into Pennsylvania. Though our lodging was a bit fancier, the Quakers took us in as they had the runaways 170 years before. Slight and winsome and sincere, gray hair about her shoulders, Gail Newbold met us at the motel. Gail is Lynn's friend and onetime roommate from Swarthmore, a college founded by the Friends. She's a member of the London Grove Meeting and was, for many years, part of the local Friday peace vigil in Kennett Square. She and her Meeting had prepared quite a day for us.

We began the morning with complimentary tickets to the lush Longwood Gardens. The vast horticultural collections and elaborate fountains of the former Du Pont estate make it a major attraction in the area. Susanna Davison picked us up from there. She has a personal connection to the freedom seekers of the eighteenth century. "Indian Deep," the farm that she and her husband purchased on Brandywine Creek, was a documented stop for freedom seekers. Susanna is a volunteer tour guide for the Kennett Underground Railroad Center. The Friends cherish their history here and keep it alive.

Susanna first took us to the Longwood Progressive Meetinghouse, site of the remarkable photograph and now the home of the Brandywine tourism office. A quilt hangs in the foyer, showing the meetinghouse and its congregation. The quilt's border portrays some of its many illustrious visitors, including Tubman, Douglass, Garrett, Sojourner Truth, and William Lloyd Garrison.

In addition to its many supporters of the Underground Railroad, Longwood Meetinghouse may have had a pivotal role in the nation's history regarding the institution of slavery. On June 20, 1862, Pennsylvania senator David Wilmot led a delegation of six Longwood members, including Thomas Garrett, to meet with President Lincoln to press their case for emancipation. This was only two months after the Battle of Shiloh, whose 23,000 casualties revealed just how deadly the Civil War had become (chapter 3.iv). Lincoln received his visitors courteously, remarking that it was a relief to meet people who were not applicants for office. One can imagine him relaxing, stretching his long legs out from behind the desk. But when he heard their plea for immediate emancipation, he seemed skeptical, noting that he could not even enforce the Constitution in the South at that time. "How would a decree of emancipation be any more effective?" he asked.[22] Yet this was plainly on his mind. Just four weeks later, he would present the first draft of the Emancipation Proclamation to his cabinet.

Susanna took us to many of the other Underground Railroad sites around Kennett Square. The Quakers were far from the only people involved. Free Black people were central to helping the enslaved find freedom, but they had to be particularly careful to leave no trace of their activities. Unlike the Quakers, they risked being sold into slavery themselves if caught. Their houses were rarely built from the brick and stone of the meetinghouses, and many have not survived.

We walked through the modest Marlborough Meetinghouse, where an Indignation Meeting was held in 1849 to protest the capture of a freedom seeker. Three years later, it was the site of a gathering that highlighted the divisions over slavery in the 1850s. Even the Quakers were far from unanimous. For some in the Meeting, the institution of slavery was simply part of the established economic system, and abolition was seen as an aggressive, worldly doctrine forced from the outside. But one Friend, Oliver Johnson, insisted on addressing the Meeting on the topic. In the tradition of silent worship, such an announced speech was considered an affront. As Johnson rose to speak, an elder directed him to sit down or leave. Another called on the constable to arrest him. Then Friends began to shake hands, the traditional signal for the end of the Meeting. Half of the Meeting departed, while the other half stayed for Johnson's address. This became known as the Marlborough Riot. Though, per the Marlborough Meeting website, it leads one to question the ability of Quakers to hold a proper riot.[23]

On our way out, an offering box stood with the caption "Donations appreciated, to be used towards the upkeep of the 1801 Meetinghouse. Thank thee." Thee donated.

The day closed with a potluck dinner at Gail's London Grove Meetinghouse, built ten years after Marlborough. The Friends wrapped us in their warm company. Aluminum foil came off an exotic Indian chickpea dish and a sturdy macaroni and cheese. The dinner crowd couldn't finish two trays of fancy brownies, and the baker insisted that we cyclists take them with us. With no room in our panniers, Lynn later gave the brownies away in the hotel elevator. After cleanup, she gave a presentation not just on the Tubman ride but on her continent-spanning peace sign. The Meeting embraced us.

Outside of London Grove stands a mammoth oak, at 82 feet one of the largest trees in the state. It's one of the few remaining Penn Oaks, believed to have been alive before William Penn first came to the New World in 1682. In this part of the country, there are people and institutions and trees that are old and noble and still standing.

The next morning brought a study in contrasts on the road to Philadelphia, from the gentle streams and covered bridges of the Brandywine Valley to the industrial landscape of the Delaware River. In sight of the Philadelphia skyline, we rode a half mile from the Philadelphia Energy Solutions refinery, largest on the East Coast. As we passed, a fifty-year-old corroded pipe in the bowels of the refinery was reaching the end of its life. Thirty-six hours later, a mushroom cloud rose as a massive explosion rocked the plant in the predawn hours. A bus-sized fragment landed across the Schuylkill River.[24] The fireball was visible from space. The blast marked the end of the site's refining operations, which had been going on there since 1866. Not everyone was sad to see it go. In a reflection of Louisiana's Cancer Alley (chapter 3.i), most of the people within a three-mile radius of the plant are people of color, and the refinery was the city's largest source of pollution. The site is being cleaned up in anticipation of the construction of a warehouse complex.[25]

In downtown Philadelphia, we searched to find the traces of William Still, by any measure a giant on the Underground Railroad. On 12th Street, his marker stands by a streetlamp in front of a brick townhouse, now a private residence. Still, a free Black man, took a job as a janitor and clerk for the Pennsylvania Anti-Slavery Society in 1847. When the Society reorganized its Vigilance Committee in 1852, he became its corresponding secretary and chairman.

Still was the key Philadelphia operative in assisting freedom seekers, sometimes hiding them in his own home. His network of conductors, including sea captains, stretched up and down the East Coast. After passage of the Fugitive Slave Law of 1850, many Underground Railroad operatives destroyed their records, lest they become evidence for prosecution. Obsessed with telling the story of the human river coming through his offices, Still kept his notes carefully hidden, forming the basis for his 1872 book, *The Underground Rail Road*. It remains the most detailed accounting of the network's operation, documenting over four hundred of the formerly enslaved received and sent on their way in the 1850s.[26]

William Still

One of those was a man named Peter, who had purchased his own freedom. In 1850 he walked into Still's office to seek assistance in retrieving his wife and children from Alabama. Still made it his job to interview each man and woman who came through. The details of Peter's story began to sound more and more familiar.

Suddenly, William looked Peter directly in the face and said, "Suppose I should tell you that I am your brother?"

Dumbfounded, Peter could only reply, "Supposin' you should?"[27]

Peter was indeed his older brother, sold south at the age of six, before William had been born. After their meeting, William brought Peter across the Delaware River to New Jersey to reunite with his mother, Charity, now eighty years old. As I would discover, Still family reunions in New Jersey go on to this day.

But more than forty years earlier, Charity Still had faced an impossible choice. She knew she could never escape from slavery with all four children. The two boys, Peter at six and Levin at eight, had the best chance of survival on their own. She kissed them as they slept and, in the words of William Still's later book, "consigned them to the hands of God." Charity and her two daughters crossed the Delaware into New Jersey, some distance downriver from where Washington crossed in 1776. The former owner, enraged at Charity's escape, quickly sold the boys to a market in Kentucky. Peter's older brother Levin died enslaved in Alabama. Peter Still resolved that he would survive and find his way to freedom, and he eventually escaped and made his way to New Jersey.

Peter's own wife and children would have a winding two-year saga ahead of them, however. Against the Still family's protestations, Peter returned to Alabama, seeking a way to buy freedom for his wife and children, but came back to Philadelphia deeply discouraged. Reading his account in the newspapers, a white abolitionist named Seth Concklin decided that he would go south to free them.

Such a journey, into the heart of the Deep South, was virtually unheard of. Yet in 1851 Concklin, posing as a laborer looking for work, made contact with Peter's family in Alabama. In the dark of night, he began rowing them in a skiff 400 miles up the Tennessee and Ohio Rivers. I know those miles well; my 2015 bike route to the west had followed these rivers (chapter 3). Concklin and the family of five made it all the way to Indiana before being captured by slave hunters and sent back south in chains. On their way back to Alabama, Concklin's body, still shackled but with the head crushed, was found in the Ohio River at Smithland, Kentucky.

The story was widely reported in the Eastern press. The publicity accomplished what Seth Concklin could not. For several years, Peter traveled to abolitionist meetings appealing for money, recounting the story of his enslavement, and Concklin's journey. By 1855, Peter had accumulated the five thousand dollars to purchase his family's freedom, and at last they came to live with him in New Jersey.[28]

Another notable visitor to William Still's office was Harriet Tubman. After her escape in 1849, Harriet blended into the large community of free Black people and freedom seekers in Philadelphia, working as a domestic and a cook. But something gnawed at her. Like Peter Still, her initial joy at achieving freedom was unsatisfying because her family remained enslaved. She described the feeling in an interview after the Civil War:

> There was no one to welcome me to the land of freedom. I was a stranger in a strange land; and my home, after all, was down in Maryland, because my father, my mother, my brothers, and sisters, and friends were there. But I was free, and they should be free.[29]

So began Harriet's amazing repeated journeys into a dangerous land. One can imagine William Still, wide-eyed, opening the door of this

Philadelphia office again and again to reveal Harriet with yet another band of freedom seekers. His book, published after the Civil War, did much to enhance Tubman's reputation, though she was already well known. He wrote:

> Harriet was a woman of no pretensions, indeed, a more ordinary specimen of humanity could hardly be found among the most unfortunate-looking farm hands of the South. Yet, in point of courage, shrewdness and disinterested exertions to rescue her fellow-men, by making personal visits to Maryland among the slaves, she was without her equal. Her success was wonderful. Time and again she made successful visits to Maryland on the Underground Rail Road, and would be absent for weeks, at a time, running daily risks while making preparations for herself and passengers. Great fears were entertained for her safety, but she seemed wholly devoid of personal fear. The idea of being captured by slave-hunters or slave-holders, seemed never to enter her mind. She was apparently proof against all adversaries.[30]

The afternoon shadows were lengthening on the streets of Philadelphia. We hurried on from Still's marker to another spot of holy ground. Mother Bethel is the first African Methodist Episcopal (AME) church in America, founded in 1791 by Richard Allen, who was once enslaved in Delaware. Four successive churches have been built on this site, the oldest parcel of land continuously owned by African Americans in the country. But we were late. Mother Bethel was already closed for the day. We were taking photographs when two women emerged from the church after locking up. They asked what we were doing, and we told them about the ride. One rolled her eyes, then waved to her friend.

"You go on, I'll let these folks in," she said. "I guess I have an appointment I'll be late for."

For our benefit only, she reopened the church, the sanctuary, and the museum, staying for the better part of an hour. The late afternoon sun streamed through the century-old stained glass windows, sermons in art. We looked up at images of stories and symbols, arks and anchors, books and tablets. In the basement museum was the first pulpit, fashioned by Richard Allen himself. An original poster from 1851, framed under glass, caught my eye:

PROCLAMATION!!
To all the Good People of Massachusetts!
Be it known that there are now three
SLAVE-HUNTERS
or
KIDNAPPERS
in Boston, looking for their prey

It went on to describe the three, including one who "looks sleepy and yet malicious. He has a Roman nose, one of his eyes has been knocked out. He looks like a Pirate, and knows how to be a Stealer of Men." We don't often get glimpses, however prejudicial, of the kind of men on Harriet's trail.

As the afternoon drifted into evening, we settled into our hotel for the night. On the skyline loomed the next morning's challenge: the massive Ben Franklin Bridge to New Jersey. This would be a crazy, full day, when all the muscles and neurons would fire, every one of them, many times. Whatever challenges these rides may present, I often think I'm most alive on tour.

Ben Franklin Bridge and Camden, New Jersey, gathering storm.

v. The Sanctuary by the Turnpike (New Jersey)

Lit up with taillights and reflective vests, we left the hotel in misty morning rush-hour traffic. The Ben Franklin Bridge has a pedestrian-bike walkway, wet and slippery in the intermittent showers. Shadowy morning light revealed only part of the bridge. The tops of the towers were lost in low clouds and drizzle. As we rode up the arc of the bridge, eight lanes rushed by to our left. To our right, 135 feet down, lay the Delaware River. We stopped at midspan to feel the shaking and pulsing of the bridge as trucks roared by. A tug and barge sailed slowly below us. It's not the place to be if one is afraid of heights.

We rolled off the bridge ramp into Camden, New Jersey. Another Still, William's great-great-grandniece, grew up on the hard streets here. Basketball was Valerie Still's escape growing up in the 1970s, but it took a while for the boys to allow her to get in the game. One day she tucked her hair up into a woolen cap to look like one of the guys, and she was selected for the pickup game. She did well. They didn't suspect that they were playing with a future member of the Women's Basketball Hall of Fame.

Valerie left Camden to go to the University of Kentucky on an athletic scholarship, leaving the university holding the all-time records for scoring and rebounding there at Lexington. She would go on to play professional basketball in the United States and in Europe, and her team would visit the Clinton White House. Back in Lexington, one of her favorite college bars was the Cheapside Bar and Grill. Only later would she discover her connection to this place. The bar is on the site of the Cheapside Auction Block, the market where traders sold her great-great-grandfather, Peter Still, and his brother Levin as young boys.[31]

Camden has changed since Valerie Still grew up there. It remains a town with a high poverty rate, and I'd long been nervous about riding through it based on Camden's difficult reputation. In 2012, it had one of the highest murder rates in the country, along with high rates of excessive force complaints against law enforcement officers. The following year, the mayor and city council dissolved the existing police department and replaced it with a countywide force with an emphasis on community policing. Homicides went down from sixty-seven in 2012 to twenty-five in 2019. Today the city is seen as a model for police reform.[32]

For us, Camden was urban riding, no more or less. It was busy, with no fancy bike paths, but far less of a problem than I'd anticipated.

Our destination, ten miles out, was a hidden sanctuary I'd driven by a thousand times, a tiny house backing to the New Jersey Turnpike.

Kings Court in Lawnside, New Jersey, seems like an ordinary suburban cul-de-sac, lined by tan and blue duplexes, the hum of the Turnpike coming through the trees. But one house is different, a two-story white clapboard structure with a chimney in the middle. Dating to around 1845, the Peter Mott House is one of the very few authentic homes left from the Underground Railroad era. Its builder, Peter Mott, was a Black farmer who helped freedom seekers along their way. Lawnside, once known as Snow Hill, is believed to be the first self-governing African American town in the North.

Our guide, Joyce Fowler, sporting short gray hair and sneakers, set aside her cane after she let us in. "I was an orphan, and this town took me in. I was adopted by a Lawnside family. You know, the town of Lawnside saved this place, too, when they were building the development," she continued. "Clarence Still, who was one of William Still's kin, actually stood in front of the bulldozer."

Joyce was right about that. His 2012 obituary tells the story of this founder of the Lawnside Historical Society, a calm, driven man who became custodian of the Still family story.[33] After the town had issued a demolition permit for the Peter Mott House, his sister-in-law Gloria said, "The most excited I ever saw Clem [Clarence Still] in my life was in 1989, when he found out it could be torn down." After stopping the bulldozer, he managed to convince the developer of the adjacent townhouses to spare it.

We live in an age where our digital footprints are everywhere, available to almost anyone. For Harriet Tubman, it was quite the opposite. She relied on stealth: no records, no traces. As one abolitionist put it at the time, "The safety of all concerned called for still tongues."[34] I asked Joyce if our famous traveler had stopped here.

"We can't say for sure that Harriet was here," she told us. "Peter Mott certainly was very much involved in the Underground Railroad, but we have no records. We would love to know for certain that she passed this way."

There was a certain way of speaking, common to both the women at Mother Bethel and Joyce Fowler. For them, it's "Harriet," like their sturdy old grandmother. It's as though the woman who'll someday be on the twenty-dollar bill is family.

We passed through Lawnside two months before their biggest event. In August, the 150th Still Family Reunion took place right across town, a giant affair with tents and a stage. The family legacy extends from a Guinean prince brought to New Jersey in 1630 through Charity's escape in the early 1800s, to her sons William and Peter, and on through doctors and musicians in the twentieth and twenty-first centuries. Valerie Still isn't the only Hall of Famer in the family. Her brother Art is in the College Football Hall of Fame and played in the National Football League. In a video from the reunion posted by Valerie, her cousin Kith looks straight into the camera and proclaims: "We are kings and queens."

We had fifty miles yet to go from Lawnside, with a marginal weather forecast. By the time we rolled north through Trenton, our cell phones were crackling out a flash flood warning. We stopped under an overpass, and I chanced to look at the Doppler radar. A big red line of storms was bearing down on us. The roadside was going to get nasty in a hurry, so I suggested a halt. We waited out a biblical downpour, rain coming down sideways, from our shelter under the bridge. I was feeling a little smug as we rode out into the late afternoon sunshine breaking through the trailing thunderheads. All clear after a perfect call.

But that same downpour had almost washed out the largely dirt and gravel Delaware and Raritan Canal Trail, our route to Princeton.

There was more water on the trail than solid ground. I couldn't believe that Lynn and Rick were following me. Then again, since New Jersey roads are notoriously busy and thin on shoulders, they didn't have much choice. We rode through quarter-mile puddles, fishtailing through the mud. We got into Princeton exhausted and with the lower half of our bikes and legs caked in dirt.

When we arrived late at the hotel, a man from maintenance was kind enough to hose off our bikes. We had no desire to go out for dinner, but the hotel bar had only curled cheese and brown grapes in little premade appetizer platters, sealed in plastic. That was okay. We packed away about a dozen.

As I lay down in bed, I could feel the blood pumping through my legs. I closed my eyes, and the images of the people and the road flashed across like the herky-jerky images of an old movie newsreel. But only briefly. Reality came unmoored, and sleep happened in seconds, easily, like freefalling into a deep, soft black pit.

vi. An Eyebrow Salon, a Subway, a Coffee Shop (New York)

New York City has its beacons of freedom—massive statues and soaring skyscrapers. I sought out a more modest collection, something akin to Morrison's benches by the road. But first we had to get there.

Lynn, Rick, and I rode across New Jersey from Princeton in a driving rain. We needed to cover forty-two miles to catch the noon ferry, the day's last crossing from the town of Highlands to Midtown Manhattan. The ferry schedule gave us no chance for a leisurely morning after the exhaustion of the previous day. Briefly, we became separated in the fog of road spray, losing time as we were forced to reestablish contact by phone. Along roads and through strip malls, our tires kicked up rooster tails behind us. My glasses kept fogging, so I ditched them. I amused myself by watching water drops roll back and forth across the front of my helmet before dropping past my nose. On the home stretch, a bike path snaked along the shore, with the Verrazzano-Narrows Bridge arching across the entrance to New York Harbor in the distance.

Breathless, we pulled into the ferry parking lot just in time. Completely soaked going up the gangway, we were looking forward to a relaxing ride into the city. We hadn't counted on full-blast air conditioning in the ferry's cabin. We froze.

Harriet came to New York by water as we did, but for us the ride into New York Harbor was a bit more majestic. The Statue of Liberty appeared out the portside window under a low gray sky. One of the first intentions for the statue was as a celebration of the abolition of slavery. Indeed, Edouard de Laboulaye, the French political thinker who first proposed the idea of a great monument as a gift from France, was cofounder of the French Anti-Slavery Society.[35] Hard to see from the ground, a broken shackle and chain lie at the statue's feet. The plaque with the Emma Lazarus paean to the immigrant—"Give me your tired, your poor . . ."—wasn't added until seventeen years after the statue's 1886 unveiling.

Yet the statue was largely rejected by Black newspapers at the time of its unveiling. At the end of Reconstruction, in 1877, as construction was starting, the shadow of Jim Crow had spread across the land. When W. E. B. Du Bois, founder of the NAACP, sailed past the statue on a return trip from Europe, he was unable to imagine the sense of hope he assumed some immigrant arrivals felt. This promise did not pertain to Black people. More recently, James Baldwin, in 1985, said that for a Black American, the Statue of Liberty is "simply a very bitter joke."[36]

One earlier protagonist in the battle for freedom had gotten a sneak peek. In 1877, after the end of his term, former president Ulysses Grant visited Frédéric-Auguste Bartholdi's workshop in Paris, where the statue was being built. History doesn't record the old man's reaction. Perhaps he reflected on the day his army had opened the passage to liberty fifteen years earlier, when his victory at Fort Donelson led to thousands of the formerly enslaved pouring across Union lines (chapter 3.iv).

For our benefit, Lady Liberty reached up and swept the rain clouds away, and the sun broke out by the time we docked at 35th Street in the heart of Manhattan. The change was abrupt. Our ride through New Jersey had been largely back roads with the occasional strip mall. Now we were literally fresh off the boat, looking up at the office towers.

After hugs on the dock, we three went our separate ways: Rick returning home to Maryland, Lynn to her daughter's family in Queens, and me to my son's family in the Bronx. Lynn and I would take a break from the bike to spend time with family, but we'd get back together for the rest of the ride to Canada. We'd miss Rick. He and I have put in a lot of miles together.

I rolled out past the United Nations, with all sorts of vehicles flying by and my personal radar on high. I felt slow and vulnerable. I'd been nervous about riding solo in Manhattan on a loaded bike. I needn't have been. Painted in green was a perfect bike lane up First Avenue. My little game was trying to time the traffic lights and anticipate when a car would be cutting in front of me. I had a tight grip on the handlebars, but the biggest concern was delivery people whizzing by on e-bikes. My grandson enjoyed spinning the crank after I arrived in the Bronx.

The next day I took a walk around lower Manhattan, trying to find one of those few places where we know that Harriet Tubman set foot during her Underground Railroad days. I knew that there wouldn't be much, that I would be looking for ghosts. But then, the freedom seekers themselves were ghosts by necessity back in the early 1800s. My guidebook was Eric Foner's *Gateway to Freedom*, a history of the Underground Railroad centered around New York City. His city map has many of the notable sites.

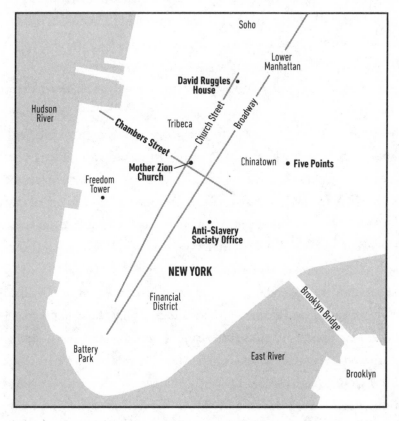

Lower Manhattan Underground Railroad sites, 1840s.

I emerged from the subway at the Brooklyn Bridge station amid the office towers of lower Manhattan. Back in Harriet's day, this was anything but a fashionable neighborhood. I sought out 142 Nassau Street, once the offices of the American Anti-Slavery Society. The building at that address today rises twelve stories. On the ground floor is an eyebrow threading salon, where a receptionist sat looking rather bored next to a row of chairs. In pre–Civil War days, Sydney Howard Gay, a white abolitionist and secretary of the Society, presided here. He was one of the few conductors (along with William Still) whose detailed records of the Underground Railroad survive. These notes proved a rich trove for Foner. By the time of Harriet's two trips through Gay's office in 1856, she was well known in abolitionist circles, for he referred to her as "Captain" in his journals.[37]

Her reputation didn't imply an easy road, even at the Anti-Slavery Society. On one visit, Harriet was trying to obtain twenty dollars to help bring her parents north from the Eastern Shore of Maryland. Initially turned down, she resolved not to eat or drink until "I get enough money to go down after the old people." She sat down on the floor where the eyebrow salon now stands, dozing on and off all day. Probably her story was whispered about in the Society office, for when she awoke, she was delighted to find that they had collected sixty dollars, while she slept, from visitors to the office.[38]

Modern-day Chinatown isn't far from Nassau Street, so I walked there for lunch, passing the august buildings of City Hall and the courthouses. My repast at a crowded, steamy dumpling shop was at the site of the notorious Five Points slum, which had its own role in Black history of the day. Charles Dickens, who had seen a few slums in his time, wrote of the Five Points in 1842: "See how the rotten beams are tumbling down, and how the patched and broken windows seem to scowl dimly, like eyes that have been hurt in drunken frays."[39]

At the time of the Civil War, the Five Points was a powder keg. Home to Irish immigrants who had borne many of the casualties in the Union ranks, the announcement of a draft lottery in 1863 brought men pouring out of the neighborhood in what became known as the Draft Riots. "Riot" is a curious term. What happened in Tulsa in 1921 used to be called a "race riot." Now it's known as the Tulsa Race Massacre. Perhaps the same terminology should be applied to New York in 1863.

After cutting the telegraph wires, the mob burned the draft office. They then turned their wrath on the city's Black citizens, whom they saw as both the cause of the war and competition for their jobs. More than a hundred died, though an accurate count was impossible. The mob even burned the Colored Orphan Asylum at 43rd Street and Fifth Avenue. The rioters ruled the city for four days, until troops just returning from the Gettysburg battlefield arrived to forcibly quell the mob.[40]

As I wandered further uptown, the towers of lower Manhattan faded to the background. At 158 Church Street is a wall of office buildings, and one has a Subway on the ground floor (the sandwich shop, not the train). Cars parked and double-parked on the busy commercial street. A cashier smoked a cigarette outside a bodega.

This is the site of the original African Methodist Episcopal Zion Church, known as Mother Zion. With Mother Bethel in Philadelphia, it was one of the first Black churches in the nation and was also prominent in the Underground Railroad. Mother Zion had a mysterious fire in 1815 but was rebuilt on the Church Street site. Its successor, built in 1925 and also known as the Freedom Church, is in Harlem. Among the celebrities who worshipped at the later Mother Zion were Langston Hughes, W. E. B. Du Bois, Marian Anderson, Joe Louis, and Paul Robeson.

It occurred to me that Frederick Douglass walked these streets. The former Mother Zion site is next to the intersection with Chambers Street. Apartment buildings fronted with fire escapes line the street today, with a patch of the Hudson just visible in the distance. In his original break for freedom in 1838, Frederick Douglass made his way up Chambers from the ferry docks, a free man for the first time. We know well his thoughts stepping off the ferry into the big city that September day, for he wrote about them:

I felt like one who had escaped a den of hungry lions. This state of mind, however, very soon subsided; and I was again seized with a feeling of great insecurity and loneliness . . . The motto which I adopted when I started from slavery was this—"Trust no man!" I saw in every white man an enemy, and in almost every colored man cause for distrust.[41]

His distrust was warranted. In the 1830s, New York City's prosperity increasingly depended on its relationship with Southern enslavers. Cotton had emerged as the nation's premier export crop, and New York merchants dominated the transatlantic trade. Southern businessmen negotiating the sales of their crops became a ubiquitous presence in the city. The sympathies extended to the political realm. As the Civil War approached, New York mayor Fernando Wood even proposed that the city itself should secede along with the South.[42] With its economy dependent on King Cotton, Gotham was fertile ground for slave hunters.

Douglass and posterity were lucky enough that he trusted the right man with his story. A Black sailor named Stewart directed him to the home of David Ruggles at 36 Lispenard Street, just nine blocks up Church Street from the site of Mother Zion. Ruggles was a Black abolitionist and secretary of the New York Vigilance Committee, which fought against the frequent kidnappings or "delivering up" of both freedom seekers and free Black people. As Douglass later wrote about Ruggles, "though watched and hemmed in on almost every side, he seemed to be more than a match for his enemies."

Douglass must have found 36 Lispenard a hive of activity. In addition to his business as a grocer, Ruggles edited the *Mirror of Liberty*, the nation's first Black-owned magazine. He would have been right at home in a Black Lives Matter protest of today, for he organized demonstrations of hundreds of Black New Yorkers outside courts where trials of the captured were underway. Amid all the bustle, Ruggles found time to help Douglass post a letter to Anna Murray, Douglass's free Black fiancée in Baltimore. On receiving the letter, she got on a train immediately and left her life behind. Anna and Frederick Douglass were married in the parlor of Ruggles's house. Ruggles then sent the couple further north, into Massachusetts, where the dangers of kidnapping would be at least reduced.

Today the building at 36 Lispenard Street has a plaque on the front identifying it as the site of an Underground Railroad station that aided over a thousand freedom seekers. Perhaps the plaque would get a nod from Toni Morrison. A coffee shop with a young upscale clientele now sits on the ground floor. I settled down to do some writing amid the ghosts and the sounds of the espresso machine. As I crossed the street to leave, I noticed the Freedom Tower in the distance and took a photograph of the two beacons, old and new.

Site of David Ruggles home, 36 Lispenard Street. A coffee shop is on the ground floor. In the distance, the Freedom Tower.

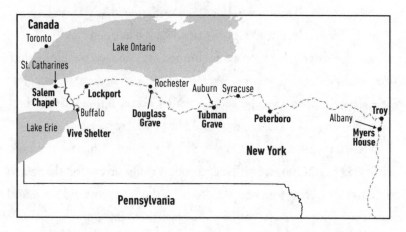

Harriet Tubman ride sites, Central New York and Ontario.

vii. Albany Vigilance (New York)

Lynn and I slipped out of New York City early on a quiet Sunday morning. My grandson was still in his pajamas when we left my son's house, where I'd stopped for a few days. Usual city traffic had vanished as we rolled up to lonely stoplights. We were bound for the Hudson Valley, with Albany three days out. We followed a route that Harriet Tubman almost certainly did not. The rail link to the capital was not in place until 1851, and before that traffic was largely by steamboat up the river. There was good reason to avoid the roads, both for Tubman and for us: the route to Albany would involve the most climbing since Cambridge.

After clearing the Bronx, we started north on a dirt trail. This turned out to be a bad idea, as we departed following a stretch of rainy days. An untold expanse of mud lay in wait, and we got a quick lesson in how to deal with fishtailing mountain bike conditions. We were about to bail out and look for another route when a young woman flew by us on skinny tires, reveling in every puddle. Suitably chastened, we wallowed through the remaining miles. Pavement finally appeared, and we were on well-paved trails for the next forty miles.

Despite that, good fortune was not to be my companion that day. I had a clumsy fall at the start of one trail, when an entrance barrier caught one of my panniers. I took the fall with a roll and ended up with a bruised ribcage. The pain never really stopped for the next 500 miles, and I assumed I had cracked a rib. I thought about seeing a doctor, but what would the medical advice be? "Can't do anything for it, but stay off the bike." So I kept pedaling and popped a lot of ibuprofen. It only hurt when I breathed.

A long day on the bike typically unfolds with many little second and third and fourth winds, and Lynn and I matched up well. She seemed to be up when I was down and vice versa. Fortunately, one of my second winds came at around mile fifty, when the steepest grades revealed themselves. We would climb almost 3,000 feet by day's end.

The next day was mercifully easier, not to say wondrous. We were bound for lunch at a restaurant at the Culinary Institute of America in Hyde Park. Converging on the restaurant were Lynn's husband, son, and daughter. The occasion was the name day of her husband's saint, San Giovanni. Needless to say, the fare was a step up from our usual roadside cuisine, with Lynn and me still in our riding apparel. No matter. The maître d' was more than welcoming. He and Giovanni discovered that they were from the same neighborhood in Italy. The conversation was in Italian and the hands flew. Giovanni poured a fragrant red from his home in Campania. A wild mushroom risotto followed tomatoes and burrata. After such a lunch, Lynn and I would both have preferred taking a nap to getting back on the bike. Somehow we managed forty miles to the town of Hudson.

More often than not, summer rain waits until the afternoon. Not so the next morning in Hudson, when we were soaked walking out the door. The rain came, on and off, for the next thirty miles. We rolled into the city of Albany and quickly got lost. The steep climb up Livingston Avenue brought us to a two-story square brick house. Was this the Stephen and Harriet Myers Residence, the restored Underground Railroad house? As Lynn and I tried to get our bearings, a car appeared out of the drizzle. The door opened, and a tall, soft-spoken Black man emerged with a bag of sandwiches.

"Would you folks care for some lunch?" Paul Stewart asked. "Lucky for you we're so busy or we would have arranged for a brass band."

We should have expected something like this. The website for Albany's Underground Railroad Education Center site, run by Paul and his wife, Mary Liz, states, "From its days as a meeting place for Albany's Vigilance Committee in the 19th century, the house on Livingston Avenue has been a place to connect with the kindness of strangers, to receive a helping hand, and to find the resources to attain freedom."

Paul brought us into the house and unfolded a table in the front room. Peeling off our jackets, we were glad to be out of the rain. Lynn and I made liberal use of Paul's paper towels to dry off. Over lunch, he began to tell us about the Underground Railroad in Albany. Details weren't easy to find, and some locals even told him, "Nothing like that happened here." Paul and Mary Liz, beginning in 1998, worked on finding the stories of the Albany Vigilance Committee. I didn't realize it at the time, but we had seen the two of them before. They were featured on the entrance video to the Harriet Tubman Center back in Maryland, part of a modern-day network of people keeping the history of the Underground Railroad alive.

Paul Stewart and the Stephen and Harriet
Myers Residence, Albany.

Paul and Mary Liz drew inspiration from the couple that lived
in the house 170 years earlier. Stephen and Harriet Myers were giants of
the Underground Railroad in New York. They assisted thousands
of individuals on the move through Albany. Stephen was a steward
on the steamboats that plied the Hudson from Albany to New York,
probably encountering many freedom seekers and directing them to his
house. He later worked full time for the Albany Vigilance Committee.
He also published the *Northern Star and Freemen's Advocate* newspaper.
In 1860, he wrote in a circular letter:

> We devote all our time to the care of the oppressed who
> come among us. Our pay is small, but yet we are willing

to continue to do what we can for them. We have arrivals every few days from southern oppression and forward them to the next depot.[43]

We know from her biographers that Harriet Tubman stayed with the Myers family when she was in Albany. As for Harriet Myers, she cared for the many runaways who came to their door during Stephen's extensive travels. We have no image of her, but a letter from her to another conductor survives:

It is hard to get mony for the fugitives it seems that Predudist against our class grows stronger every day and yet we have a few good friends that feel for the Bleeding slave that comes Pantting at their doors. [44]

In a corner behind us, dominating the room, stood a tall mixed-media sculpture of copper, wood, ceramic tile, and beads. Next to it hung fourteen photographs of ornate wooden boxes. I asked Paul about it.

"Well, there's a story there," he said.

In 2005, during excavation for a sewer project in the nearby area known as Schuyler Flatts, workers came upon human remains. They had uncovered the unmarked burial ground once used by people enslaved by the prominent colonial Schuyler family.

Prior to the American Revolution, the institution of slavery was widespread in New York. Between 1700 and 1774, over seven thousand of the enslaved were imported into New York City, most to be sold in the surrounding rural areas. Auctions took place regularly at a market on Wall Street. But the Revolution brought a dramatic change. For most of the war, New York City was held by the British, who offered freedom to those enslaved to weaken the revolutionary cause. The city became a haven for freedom seekers. When the British sailed off in 1783, they took over three thousand Black people with them, a fact that incensed General Washington. The exodus included a married couple that he had once enslaved at Mount Vernon.[45] Nevertheless, slavery continued at Schuyler Flatts until at least 1800, the date of the last recorded purchase of a human there. This is the approximate era from which the remains originate.

What followed the excavation crew's discovery was an eleven-year saga. Paul explained the debate over how the remains should be handled.

"The folks from the New York State Museum were willing to do an analysis of the bones," he said, "but they waited for the community to come forward. There was one clear perspective that the remains were sacred and should be reburied untouched. The other view was that these people would want something of their story to be told. We put together a Re-Burial Committee. We decided that we should let the bones speak."

They spoke indeed. Of the fourteen enslaved people buried there, five died in infancy and two others before the age of ten. Bones of the other seven told of a lifetime of brutal work, with early-onset arthritis and musculoskeletal stress. DNA analysis revealed that one of them had come from Madagascar and others from West Africa, a source for the Hudson Valley slave trade during the late eighteenth century. And a surprise: one of the women had descended from the Micmac people in the Canadian Maritimes. The Re-Burial Committee contacted the Micmac to ensure proper burial rites. The archaeology also produced a startling image: the reconstructed face of one of the enslaved women.[46] The image of a face must have changed the discussion. Suddenly these were not bones in a graveyard but the face of someone who could have lived down the street.

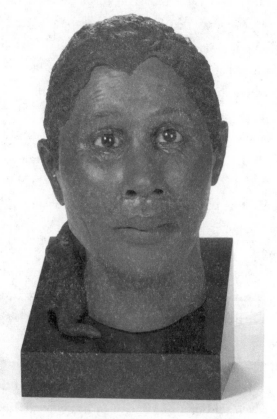

Face without a name: Reconstruction of one of the enslaved women from Schuyler Flatts.

The Re-Burial Committee then considered how best to celebrate the lives of these anonymous people. They put out a call to the community to create ossuaries, small wooden coffins. The ossuaries were to be decorated with a theme incorporating the Sankofa, the Akan West African symbol portraying a bird looking back, meaning "it is not wrong to retrieve what you have lost or forgotten."

The Sankofa symbol.

The response was overwhelming. Designs were submitted by local artists, including fourth-grade students. Volunteers from the Northeastern Woodworkers Association built the elegant ossuaries, made of tulip poplar with mortise edges and redwood spline joints. An artist from Philadelphia, Deedee McCullough, produced "The Free Wall," the great copper sculpture now at the Myers House, as a memorial to the fourteen.[47]

"She drove it up from Philly in her small car the day of the memorial," Paul said. "We weren't even sure how we would get it out."

Paul was one of the organizers of the memorial. On June 16, 2016, the fourteen ossuaries and their passengers lay in state at the Schuyler Mansion, beneath a portrait of General Philip Schuyler, the family patriarch and Revolutionary War hero whose family once enslaved them. They lay just a few paces from where Alexander Hamilton married the general's daughter Eliza in 1780, in a scene celebrated in the musical *Hamilton*. The fourteen were buried at the St. Agnes Cemetery in the town of Menands.

After we visited Albany, Paul sent me a photograph of Dan Hogan, an artist who made two of the ossuaries, and Evelyn King, chair of the Re-Burial Committee. I had trouble getting the image out of my head:

Dan's tattooed hand and Evelyn's thoughtful gaze. What the people of Albany did does not atone for what began with horrors in villages in Madagascar and West Africa, whose aftershocks continue to this day. But it is a light that shines. Black and white people, artists and scientists, community leaders and the community itself faced a hard situation and, over the course of a decade, found a way to honor the people carried away so long ago.

Lynn and I rolled down the hill from the Myers Residence and found the start of the Erie Canal along the Hudson River in Albany. The Canal's opening, in 1825, dramatically lowered the cost of moving goods from the West and led to the industrialization and growth of cities and towns across New York State and through the Great Lakes to the nation's heartland. Our next destination, eight miles up the river, was the city of Troy. In 1860, Troy was one of the richest cities in the United States and became the site of one of Harriet Tubman's most dramatic rescues.

Lynn and I spun around and around Troy looking for the marker we had read about. None of the locals seemed to know about it. Then, on the side of a building, we found a bronze plaque:

HERE WAS BEGUN
APRIL 27, 1860
THE RESCUE OF CHARLES NALLE
AN ESCAPED SLAVE WHO HAD BEEN ARRESTED
UNDER THE FUGITIVE SLAVE ACT

Charles Nalle escaped from Culpeper, Virginia, in 1858 and found refuge and work in Troy. But not safety. Under the Fugitive Slave

Act, the escaped could be tracked anywhere in the country. Charles's enslaver—and half brother—Blucher Hansbrough received word of Charles's presence in Troy and sent a slave hunter, armed with a warrant, to retrieve him. While on his way to a bakery, Charles was grabbed, put in chains, and led to the building where we saw the plaque, then the Office of the United States Commissioner.

Troy had an active Vigilance Committee and Underground Railroad presence. Troy was also the home of several of Harriet Tubman's relatives, including Kessiah Bowley, her niece whom she had helped rescue off the auction block in Cambridge (chapter 2.i). Harriet happened to be visiting her Troy family. Following Charles's kidnapping, the Vigilance Committee sprang into action. Harriet heard the commotion outside the customhouse and joined in the growing crowd.

Tubman was small, remarkably strong, and—to the white marshals—easy to overlook, attributes that she used to her benefit in the next few minutes. She put on a sunbonnet, stooped over in the manner of an old woman, and slipped up the stairs to the room next to where Nalle was being held. As Nalle was led out in chains between a phalanx of marshals, Tubman yelled to the crowd from the upstairs window: "Here he comes—take him!" She then ran down the stairs and wrapped her arms around Nalle. In the melee, she held on to him even as her outer clothes and shoes were torn off.

The Vigilance Committee supporters managed to extract Nalle and put him on a skiff to row across the Hudson to West Troy (now Watervliet). The constable in West Troy recaptured Nalle, but the crowd re-formed and used a battering ram to break down the door of the police station. Finally Charles Nalle made good his escape to the town of Amsterdam. The citizens of Troy and West Troy then gathered contributions to legally buy his freedom for $650. Tubman proceeded on her travels to a hero's welcome at abolitionist meetings in Boston, where the story of the Troy rescue had made national news. [48]

A few weeks after the rescue, Charles's wife, Kitty, and their children arrived in Troy from Washington, after being separated from Charles for more than four years. After the Civil War, the family settled back in Washington. One of their children, John Nalle, would grow up to become one of the first Black superintendents of the District of Columbia Public Schools and the namesake of a DC elementary school.

The next spring, after our ride through New York, Lynn and Rick and I rode by the leafy neighborhood of the Rock Creek Cemetery in Washington. Charles Nalle came to rest here in 1875. Though a substantial contingent of the Nalle family is buried here, Charles's grave was apparently disturbed by highway excavation at some point. [49] But the family is in good company. Right down the street is the cottage that was President Lincoln's retreat during much of the Civil War.

I was still obsessed by Nalle's saga three years after the original ride through Troy. As I read more into his story, I realized that he had been enslaved not so far from where I lived. So it came to pass that Lynn and I rode near Culpeper in the middle of a 70-mile day, looking to find the place where Blucher Hansbrough held his half brother Charles Nalle in bondage. On a prominent ridge east of town, we parked the bikes on a gate marked "No Trespassing" by the American Battlefield Trust. The Trust had given us permission to enter this now-overgrown hillside. For Hansbrough's Ridge, site of the plantation, has its own history. In the winter of 1863–64, it was the winter camp of the Army of the Potomac and its newly appointed commander, General Grant. Over the years traveling Freedom Road, I would encounter Ulysses Grant again and again.

I walked up the ridge with Lynn and with Concetta, who had been driving support for us. The trail hadn't been easy to find. The first road to the ridge shown on Google Maps turned out to be a soybean field. In the thick midday heat, we made false turn after false turn on rutted gravel roads. Finally, just off the main road, I caught sight of the Trust's sign. We made our way past the gate up a path through second-growth forest. Nothing remains of the plantation. We walked to a place where we could look out on the Virginia Piedmont laid out below us. Off in the distance, the great blue shoulders of what is now Shenandoah National Park filled the horizon. We weren't the first to take in this vista. On New Year's Day 1864, a young private from Waterloo, New York, wrote to his sister:

> "The view from our camp is magnificent. We are on the top of an exceeding high hill from whence we can look down upon the canvas cities of the Army of the Potomac on almost every side. Off to the west, nestling among the hills, the city of Culpepper can be seen—its bright spires looking still brighter against the dark background of the Blue Ridge whose towering peaks and cliffs are now covered with snow."[50]

"Canvas cities" was no exaggeration. Hansbrough's Ridge was part of the 120,000-soldier winter encampment of the Army of the Potomac. Its presence was well documented. In photographs of the time, one can almost smell the smoke rising from campfires and hear the neighing of horses. There's a certain camaraderie and warmth to the image of cold camp life in the army's hilltop fortress. Two and a half years into the war, the young men must have carried a quiet dread of the coming spring and the campaign from which many of them would not return.

*Members of the 18th Pennsylvania Cavalry Regiment pose
in their camp, with horse saddles and newly built winter
huts, in February 1864 on Hansbrough's Ridge.*

Today the woods have reclaimed the encampment, but faint trench lines still run through the forest. Hansbrough's Ridge is sometimes known as the Union's Valley Forge.[51] In May of 1864, the Union Army broke camp there to deliver the final blows that would finish the Confederacy: the Wilderness, Spotsylvania, North Anna, Cold Harbor, Petersburg. The winter before, the gray eyes of Ulysses Grant had looked out from where Charles Nalle had been enslaved to the sites of the battles to come.

viii. The Gossamer Mansion (New York)

Once upon a time, there lived a wealthy man, patron of noble but seemingly impossible causes. Gerrit Smith and his great white beard presided from a massive columned mansion over the little town of Peterboro, New York. Prominent among his causes was the abolition of slavery. In 1848, as was often the case, two of the formerly enslaved were staying in Peterboro. Frederick Douglass wrote a letter warning of slave hunters coming after them, suggesting that they needed to be on the move. Henry Highland Garnet, another prominent abolitionist who was with them at the time, wrote back: "There are yet two places where slaveholders cannot come: Heaven and Peterboro." After our day's steep climb out of the Mohawk Valley, we would reach the latter and seemingly be just short of the former.

Lynn and I were westbound from Troy to this mansion on the hill, an epicenter in the battle for a nation's soul, which drew abolitionists and freedom seekers in the decades before the Civil War. We picked up the Erie Canalway Trail, a beautiful bike path through the Mohawk Valley. Old locks and aqueducts, remnants of nineteenth-century glory, are scattered along the trail. The Canal was central to the development of the Industrial Revolution in the United States. With its opening, the products of the West were linked to the markets of the East. Towns along the Canal grew and thrived. The town at the ultimate seaward end, New York City, boomed.

In Schenectady we again became three, as my friend of a half century, Jan Kublick, joined us for several days. He retains the angular face and build of the undersized small-town quarterback he once was. We rolled through his hometown, Mohawk, quintessential rural America: churches and ice cream shop, American Legion Hall and abandoned clothing factory. I have a little history here, too. Once when rebuilding a Volkswagen in his parents' driveway. I left a socket wrench on the engine on first restarting. I was pleased that it fired up but saw the wrench fly over the neighbor's house out of the corner of my eye.

Fortunately, no one was home. Over the years, I went to Jan's wedding and several family funerals at Blessed Sacrament Church. His mom and dad and first wife rest up the hill. "Lot of ghosts here," he said.

The Erie Canalway has a certain grace to it. One church put out coolers of ice water and opened its restrooms to cyclists. Not surprisingly for a canal, there are few hills. For riders, it's a joy: rolling from one little town to another, stopping off on the patios of trailside restaurants. These days the Canal holds mostly pleasure boats with only an occasional tug. But I fulfilled a bucket list item: after seeing us, a tug blew its whistle as we rode by.

Out on the straight stretches, Lynn gave us a lesson in pace lines, where riders take advantage of each other's shelter from the wind. One rider takes the hard pull in front, breaking the wind, while the others tuck down into the slipstream. We don't take identical intervals at the front, she said: "Pull as long as you feel up to it, then drop back. It's not a competition, there's no even weighting. Each pulls according to her or his ability." We barreled down the trail, all in line. In my head, the musical accompaniment was Duke Ellington's "Take the A Train."

We rode through Ilion, the last town on the Canal before the big climb out of the Mohawk Valley. In planning the ride, this one stood out on the elevation profile as the longest and steepest from Maryland to Ontario. We turned south, taking on the steady ascent up Ilion Gorge. The main climb wasn't quite as steep as I'd imagined, but once out of the valley, some inclines later in the day hit 13 percent. Jan, Lynn, and I were all feeling the heat. I slowed down to try to keep moving, to maintain a steady uphill pace while keeping my heart from banging out of my chest.

We'd make forty-four miles that day. Back in the 1840s, a ride of a quarter of that distance could take all day. Gerrit Smith wrote of a trip back home to Peterboro where the stagecoach got stuck multiple times, and the passengers had to walk ten miles in the night "in deep wind . . . my shoes and stockings were continually soaked."[52] Of course, passengers on the Underground Railroad rarely had the benefit of stagecoaches, or even shoes.

I'd spent some time anticipating Peterboro. I'd corresponded with Norman Dann, a retired professor who wrote an extensive biography of Gerrit Smith and is a docent at the Gerrit Smith Estate National Historic Landmark. His wife, Dot Willsey, is the president of the National Abolition Hall of Fame, located in the old Peterboro church where the inaugural meeting of the New York State Anti-Slavery Society was held in 1835. As Lynn and Jan and I rode into town on a bright summer day, a gray eminence in khaki shorts with glasses hanging from his neck walked across the village green. Professor Dann, I presume.

Gerrit Smith, right, and his biographer, Norman Dann.
A photograph of the Smith mansion is in the background.

Like Paul and Mary Liz Stewart in Albany, Norm and Dot seemed to know the long-dead heroes of the Underground Railroad personally. They walked us into a town from another time, Gerrit Smith's domain. One of the richest men in the country, Smith had inherited a fortune from his father's stake in the John Jacob Astor fur empire, then invested in real estate. He also inherited a grand five-column mansion off the green in Peterboro. He hosted hundreds of guests, an average of thirty-three per month, and many were travelers on the Underground Railroad. I wandered across an expanse of lawn looking for this amazing mansion but found only a historical marker. The great house burned in 1936. All that remains is the space where the mansion rested, but one can imagine its gossamer outlines.

Early on, Gerrit Smith resolved to use his vast fortune in the service of social reform. One might see a present-day reflection in activist and philanthropist Tom Steyer. Smith's passions included not just abolition but also women's rights. Elizabeth Cady Stanton, Lucretia Mott, and Susan B. Anthony were all visitors to Peterboro. For his radical views, Smith was often referred to as "crazy" in local papers, yet he was elected to Congress in 1852.[53] His philosophy was not completely out of touch with the local community. So many fiery sermons of preachers and reformers lashed Central New York in the early 1800s that it became known as the "Burned-Over District." In keeping with this tradition, Smith was one of the founders of the Liberty Party, a precursor to the Republican Party. In an 1861 speech, he said, "Life is short. Let us hasten to say what we believe men need to have said, even though we shall be hated for saying it."[54]

His most important contributions were to the abolitionist cause. Everyone who was anyone in the movement came to Peterboro. Frederick Douglass would dedicate his autobiography to Smith. Nikole Hannah-Jones, who created *The 1619 Project*, might have been speaking of him: "Even at the darkest moments in this country, there was also always a biracial, sometimes a multiracial group of citizens, who are pushing for it to be better, who were fighting for this country to live up to its highest ideals."[55]

On the eve of the passage of one of the nation's most infamous laws, Douglass and Smith presided over a gathering of fifty of the formerly enslaved and two thousand of their white supporters in nearby Cazenovia for the Anti-Fugitive Slave Law Convention. A faded daguerreotype from the convention's last day shows Smith with Douglass, together with a who's who of abolitionists of the day.

Daguerreotype of the Anti-Fugitive Slave Law Convention, Cazenovia, New York, August 1850. Gerrit Smith (beardless) stands in the center, hand raised. Seated in front of Smith is Frederick Douglass. At Smith's left, in a bonnet, is Mary Edmonson, while her sister Emily is at Smith's right.

Two special guests grace the image. On either side of Gerrit Smith, in bonnets, stand Emily and Mary Edmonson, who had quite a dramatic journey to reach Cazenovia. The Edmonson sisters grew up enslaved where a golf course now stands, three miles from my home in Maryland. In 1848, as thirteen- and fifteen-year-olds, they hid aboard the schooner *Pearl* with seventy-four other freedom seekers, leaving Washington to sail down the Potomac River in an audacious flight from bondage. But the *Pearl* was a sailing ship, and their enslavers quickly commandeered a steam vessel to track them down. The *Pearl* made it only as far as the mouth of the Potomac, where it was captured and towed back to Washington. After being paraded through the streets of the capital, the Edmonson sisters were shipped in the hold of the brig *Union* to the slave markets of New Orleans.[56]

Unlike the other passengers of the *Pearl*, they had hope. Their father, who was free, approached an abolitionist congressman, Joshua Giddings, desperately seeking his help. The Edmonson sisters were devout Christians, and their fate became a cause célèbre for the religious abolitionist community. Giddings contacted none other than the Rev. Henry Ward Beecher, brother to Harriet Beecher Stowe, who thundered from his Brooklyn, New York, pulpit, raising the money to purchase their freedom. Meanwhile, the slave traders, sensing a payday, shipped the sisters back north to Alexandria, Virginia, where they were held in slave pens. The payment of $2,250 (roughly $60,000–80,000 in today's dollars) was delivered to Alexandria by one William Chaplin, an associate of Gerrit Smith and planner of the *Pearl* escape. It wouldn't be his last anti-slavery escapade in the Washington area.

Suddenly the Edmonson sisters were not just free, but celebrities. Emily would ultimately speak—and sing—at abolitionist meetings across the North, including Cazenovia.[57] Harriet Beecher Stowe, using her newfound wealth from *Uncle Tom's Cabin*, sponsored their education. The sisters spent a year at New York Central College, an institution in McGrawville (now McGraw) with the then-revolutionary practice of admitting Black students. They then moved to Oberlin College in Ohio. Throughout their ordeals of slave pens, slave ships, and auction rooms, the girls had been lucky in one regard: they had stayed together. At Oberlin, that changed. Mary Edmonson died of tuberculosis there at the age of twenty.

After the grief and loneliness of losing her sister, Emily Edmonson couldn't stay at Oberlin. But the abolitionists sought her help. Myrtilla Miner, a teacher in the anti-slavery hotbed of Macedon, New York, had been given the task of opening a school in the District of Columbia with the goal of training African American women to become teachers. With the urging and sponsorship of Harriet Beecher Stowe, Emily moved back to Washington to work at Miner's school, also reuniting with her parents. The Miner School for Colored Girls in Washington ultimately became DC Teachers College, which was later incorporated into the University of the District of Columbia. Emily became a lifelong neighbor and friend of the Lion of Anacostia, Frederick Douglass.[58] She was fifteen when she appeared in the Cazenovia daguerreotype with him. She died in 1895, at the age of sixty, the same year as Douglass.

I found myself following the women in the bonnets from the North to the South. After visiting Peterboro and Cazenovia on the Harriet Tubman ride, I returned to learn the Edmonson sisters' story. I pushed the button on the video doorbell of the elementary school in McGraw, New York, and the secretary buzzed me in. She directed me to a rusty historical marker for New York Central College, "DEDICATED TO EQUALITY AND BROTHERHOOD." "The kids don't realize what happened in our little town," she said.

When we came back to the Washington area, Lynn Salvo set up a series of bike trips dedicated to the *Pearl* saga. She led us to the

Maryland golf course, the site of the sisters' childhood home. Another expedition took us to the Miner Teachers College Building, the 1913 successor to the original "School for Colored Girls." But the pilgrimage that sticks in my mind was a ride to Alexandria. On a busy street of office buildings and grocery stores is the site of the Bruin and Hill slave pens, where the Edmonson sisters were held. Their likeness is in bronze there. On the back of the sculpture is a tiny image of the *Pearl*, on whose decks they once sailed away.

Edmonson Sisters Sculpture and Historical Marker, Alexandria, Virginia.

The Edmonson sisters aren't the only Peterboro connection to the Washington area. On August 8, 1850, in advance of the Anti-Fugitive

Slave Law Convention, the abolitionists planned another audacious move. In the dead of night, a carriage crossed out of the District of Columbia into Maryland. It was driven by William Chaplin, a prominent member of the Albany Vigilance Committee and architect of the *Pearl* escape attempt. The passengers in the carriage were two men enslaved by Southern senators. Allen, whose last name is not recorded, was on the run from Sen. Alexander Stephens of Georgia, who would later be vice president of the Confederacy. Garland White was escaping from Sen. Robert Toombs, also of Georgia.

A posse caught up with the carriage at the state line, but in a stark difference from most Underground Railroad captures, the freedom seekers were armed. Twenty-seven shots were fired before they realized they were trapped. The briefly freed men were returned to the senators and quickly sold, though White would later escape again to serve as a chaplain with the US Colored Troops in the Civil War. Chaplin was locked up in the jail in Rockville, Maryland—my hometown—with bail set at the then-astounding sum of $19,000. Gerrit Smith put up most of the bail, and Chaplin fled north, never to stand trial. A historical marker now stands at the District of Columbia line at the site of the shootout.[59]

Harriet Tubman, ever indefatigable, came to know Peterboro well, with at least two documented visits with freedom seekers and likely many more. In Peterboro, she was over 600 miles from home, virtually all on foot. She saw the Smith mansion as both an important station on the Underground Railroad and a place for rest and refuge. During one stay, Smith's son postponed a hunting trip to go to the village to buy her a pair of shoes. She met with Smith and John Brown in Peterboro and discussed the Harpers Ferry plan.[60] In January 1861, Smith wrote that Tubman "sits by my side. . . . She returned from another of her southern expeditions, bringing with her seven slaves," having "badly frosted" her feet.[61] After the Civil War, when Tubman was having difficulty supporting herself financially, Smith underwrote the cost of printing her memoirs so that she would have a source of income.[62]

Although the Smith mansion is no longer standing, Norm led us to the place where he feels closest to the Underground Railroad. He had set up folding chairs in an old stable where the musty smell of horses seemed to emanate from the wood. White paint peeled from the walls and vanished completely where the horses once rubbed against their stalls. So many footsteps and hooves had paced the wooden floor that the sharp edges of the floorboards were rounded off. Norm leaned forward from his chair, extended his hand, and looked at each of us, one by one. He said:

> This is one of the few places where an original Underground Railroad stable still exists. Here, Gerrit's horses and wagons were ready to take runaways on the last leg, to the docks that he owned in Oswego, where his ships would take them to Canada. Imagine if you were a runaway, three or four months on the trail, drinking out of streams. What would you feel looking on the horse that would take you to freedom? I've had people visit this place with tears in their eyes. We can read the facts. Try to feel this place.

For decades, Smith had fought for abolition through speeches, political action, and philanthropy, not to mention his role on the Underground Railroad. But by the 1850s, he was growing weary with the lack of progress on emancipation. He found himself drawn to a man of action. More and more frequently, another man with a great long beard came to visit Peterboro.

John Brown had a certain appeal. His was the visage of an Old Testament prophet, the man who would grab this evil of slavery in his hands and smash it, as Malcolm X would say a hundred years later, "by any means necessary." Brown's opinion of Gerrit Smith was restrained: "a little naive, a somewhat open and pleasant country gentleman who could afford to subsidize his own opinions."[63] He would support more than opinions. Smith would later be revealed as the leader of the Secret Six, Northern abolitionists who would bankroll Brown's battles against enslavers in Kansas and beyond. Smith would purchase the farm in the Adirondacks that he called Timbuktoo, where John Brown, Lewis Leary, and other Harpers Ferry raiders would come to rest (chapter 3.xi).

We left Peterboro by car, driven by an old cycling friend. Many years before I rode across the United States, Ed Hillenbrand had done the same thing and later told me of the magical springs high on an Idaho pass. I had completely forgotten about them until a woman at the campground off Lolo Pass asked, "You know about the hot springs, don't you?" This night, Ed drove us to a slightly more civilized affair. Jan loaned me a fleece for a cool June evening at his house, high on a ridgeline above the little town of Tully. Old friends from Tully and seemingly endless bottles of wine greeted Lynn and me around a big glass table, as stars gradually revealed themselves. Seven hundred miles down the road, we were very close to home.

Jan ferried us back to Peterboro the next morning to continue riding. Before we left by bike, I took a last walk across the lawn of the gossamer mansion in the morning dew. Here, in blowing snow on February 23, 1858, Gerrit Smith paced with Franklin Sanborn, a prominent Boston abolitionist, trying to decide whether they would support lighting the match that would lead to the Civil War. An anxious John Brown waited inside. Brown got the answer he wished for.

A year and a half later, a letter and a bank draft from Gerrit Smith to John Brown would be found after Brown's capture following the raid on Harpers Ferry, Virginia.

ix. Two Cemeteries (New York)

Harriet Tubman and Frederick Douglass grew up enslaved on adjacent peninsulas of the Chesapeake Bay, only forty-two miles apart by wagon on Maryland's Eastern Shore. As an adult, she of quiet, boundless courage, illiterate, kept by necessity the lowest of profiles. He of thundering eloquence, author of three autobiographies, was easily the most well known African American of his age. After the whirlwinds that were their lives, they would both come to rest in Central New York, just sixty-four miles apart. Or, by other measures, a day's bike ride.

On a cool, gray morning, Lynn and I rolled downhill out of Peterboro to the Canalway. We rode west to Syracuse and Auburn, a sixty-mile ride, then on to Rochester the following morning. Riding out of Peterboro felt like another homecoming in a couple of ways. After a 723-mile trip, we would arrive at the Harriet Tubman Home in Auburn, where, after many journeys and thousands of miles on foot, Harriet brought her family to live. And Concetta rejoined us, carrying gear and supporting Lynn and me for the rest of the trip.

We had a quiet, flat morning on the Erie Canalway bound for Syracuse, dodging flocks of geese, downy goslings with hissing moms. When a support vehicle wasn't around, I carried a couple of big panniers on my heavy steel Trek. I also carried a big tool kit, prepared for most roadside breakdowns. Lynn traveled light on a carbon fiber Cannondale, with two microscopic bags and only basic tools for a flat. Rick and I always wondered just what she carried in her bags when life was reduced to its absolute minimum. But traveling light is her style. She doesn't ride fast, but she can ride forever.

Between Peterboro and Rochester, a powerful source of support for the Underground Railroad had developed in the 1840s and '50s in rapidly industrializing Central New York. We were approaching Syracuse, one of the epicenters of that support, what Daniel Webster called "that laboratory of abolitionism, libel, and treason."[64] He was one of the architects of the Compromise of 1850, which included the Fugitive Slave Law. Webster thought this would be the deal that would keep the Union together, and that it might just be his ticket to the White House. On a Syracuse side street, the balcony still stands where Webster, in 1851, roared to the populace that "the law must be executed, not only in carrying back the slave, but against those guilty of treasonable practices in resisting its execution."[65] One of those treasonous souls responded. In a thunderous speech, Frederick Douglass responded that the law had transformed "your broad republican domain into a hunting-ground for men."[66]

But the true response to Daniel Webster came with action and not words. Lynn and I rode into downtown Syracuse, on the hunt for traces of that action. At lunchtime in Clinton Square, several bands were setting up for a music festival. Sound checks from the stage echoed off buildings. We expected to find an obscure plaque on the side of a building. Yet we found ourselves sitting on a curb eating street food next to a striking monument to the events of October 1, 1851.

William "Jerry" Henry had escaped from slavery in Missouri and settled in presumably safe Syracuse. But in 1851, not long after Webster's speech, a slave hunter, accompanied by federal marshals, burst into his workshop, manacled him, and dragged him to the city jail. Meanwhile, word of the rendition got out to attendees of the convention of the abolitionist Liberty Party, chaired by Gerrit Smith and taking place in Syracuse at the same time. Triggered by the alarm, church bells began to ring across the city. A crowd of hundreds, led by Black abolitionist Jerome Longuen, stormed the jail and put Henry in a carriage bound for Canada, safety, and freedom.

For many years afterward, abolitionists would gather in Syracuse on October 1st to celebrate the Jerry Rescue.[67] The site of the jail was across the street from our roadside lunch spot, where an ice cream shop occupies the ground floor of an office building. In the swelling crowd for the music festival was perhaps an echo of the multitude who gathered across from the jail that day in October. *You won't take him from us. Not here, not in this place.* Frozen in bronze above our heads was a city's finest hour: vivid running figures, one with broken shackles on his arms.

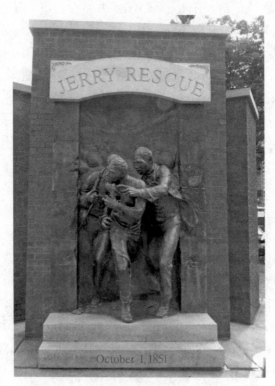

Jerry Rescue Monument, Syracuse, New York.

Our time in Syracuse was short, for we still had thirty miles to go to Auburn, our destination for the night. In 1859, Harriet Tubman bought a house and a parcel of land there from abolitionist William Seward, then a senator and soon to be Lincoln's secretary of state. It became her family home, and she later established and operated a home for the elderly on the lot. Today both houses survive, together with a visitor center. I'd arranged a visit with one of the docents for that afternoon.

The passage from Syracuse wasn't to be easy. Climbing a hill in the heat on busy US Route 20, I heard the telltale hiss of a flat tire, my first of the trip. Suddenly our appointment with the docent was in jeopardy. I tried to change the tire as fast as I could. Trucks roared by as I sat in the roadside grit amid cigarette butts, prying the tire bead off the rim and pulling out the old tube. I carelessly slapped in a new tube and remounted the tire. Sweat was dripping into the sand as I struggled with the small frame pump, but a hiss again came from the tire. After several frustrating tries, I found the culprit: a tiny wire buried in the tread, a remnant of the disintegration of a car's steel-belted radial tire long ago. We were finally back on the road. Lynn said she didn't realize I possessed that kind of language.

We finally rolled into Auburn late in the afternoon, not a little hot under the collar, and made the turn into the Harriet Tubman National Historical Park. Mike Long, our guide, graciously stayed late to escort us. He had been instrumental in getting the visitor center built. Harriet's life is laid out in panels, drawings, and photographs. Outside, her Home for the Aged has been restored, and we were able to walk through it. Across the way, her red brick house still stands, but with much restoration work to do. To our disappointment, visitors were not yet allowed to enter.

Concetta, Lynn, and I set out the next morning to find Harriet. We rolled past two stone pillars through the entrance to Auburn's Fort Hill

Cemetery. A damp, dewy morning brought us down winding pathways smelling of moss, through a forest of headstones. Though we had a map, we were quite lost. And then, under a great old evergreen, there she was. We had already driven by once because the stone was not very big. Lynn said later, "We finally caught up with her, but only because she stopped."

Harriet had traveled a long way from the Brodess Farm. She had made the same journey as we had, many times, under the most hazardous of conditions. I didn't quite feel entitled to my weariness. Her resting place is modest, surrounded by family, as one might expect. Later in life, Harriet fell in love with and married a man staying at her home, Nelson Davis, and she took his name. The simple stone reads HARRIET TUBMAN DAVIS.

At the gravesite, I felt the power in that modesty. She let her actions speak. Though she would become a sought-after speaker and an advocate for women's rights and those of the newly freed, maintenance of her image was never a concern. She might have commanded monuments in her time, but she did not pursue any particular recognition. She allowed us to discover her acts, and in that discovery, her image has only grown with the more than a century since her passing. Miles Davis said, "It's not the notes you play. It's the notes you don't play."

Harriet Tubman grave, Fort Hill Cemetery, Auburn, New York.

Next to her marker sits a faded brass star inscribed with US VET-
ERAN. That she was, in yet another of her lives. Harriet Tubman was
never paid a soldier's pension, though she surely deserved one. In
1863, under the command of Colonel James Montgomery, Tubman
led an expedition of three gunboats up the Combahee River of South
Carolina, where they routed rebel forces, freed over seven hundred of
the enslaved, and destroyed stockpiles of food and munitions.

We each laid a hand on the stone and then went on our way. Lynn
and I had a gentle fifty-mile ride through marshlands on the north ends
of the Finger Lakes, while Concetta spent the day at the Montezuma
National Wildlife Refuge gathering images of hawks at play in the sky.
We rejoined at a motel outside Rochester. About an hour later, Lynn
brought us down to the lobby to meet Jerry Sparmann, an outgoing,
bearded man, the brother of one of Lynn's close friends.

"My girlfriend and I would like to take you around Rochester
and have dinner later," he said. "We could stop by and pick her up at
her studio. She does stained glass." Which was kind of like saying
Leonardo da Vinci does pictures. Valerie O'Hara is the third generation to run the Pike Stained Glass Studios, in the family since 1908.
She is animated, passionate, down to earth, funny. And an amazing
talent.

"Not too many churches in upstate New York that we don't have
work in," she said.

On a Sunday afternoon she walked us around the busy, cluttered
studio where she was working. On the walls hung photographs of
all styles of stained glass, including a window at the Princeton Chapel.
She led us to her light table and her current project, restoring an
original hundred-year-old Tiffany glass piece. Concetta is a stained
glass hobbyist.

"Can I touch it?" she asked.

Valerie smiled and nodded. The next day we would stop to see her fourteen windows at the St. Basil Chapel on the campus of St. John Fisher College, great soaring modern splashes of color. To paraphrase Wren's epitaph, if you seek her legacy, look around you.

Valerie O'Hara at her light table, Pike Stained Glass Studios, Rochester.

Valerie closed up shop, and we piled into Jerry's car to see the sights of their city. Our first stop was the Susan B. Anthony House. Anthony and Frederick Douglass were colleagues and friends for many years. Indeed, Douglass spoke at the 1848 Seneca Falls women's rights convention. In a park up the street, a statue of the two of them, seated, deep in conversation, arrests the eye. Its title: *Let's Have Tea.*

One might expect to see a Frederick Douglass House in his adopted town, where he published the *North Star* newspaper for many years. But in 1872, while he was away in Washington after the war, his farm home, where many groups of freedom seekers had gained refuge, burned to the ground. In all likelihood, it was arson. Douglass and his family moved to Washington, where he held a number of government posts and continued an active speaking schedule. In preparing for this trip, Rick Sullivan and I rode our bikes from our houses in Maryland to visit the home that Douglass called Cedar Hill, now a National Historic Site. It sits on a high bluff across the river with a perfect view of Washington and the Capitol. In later years, his great white mane gave him one of his many monikers: the Lion of Anacostia.

But Rochester did not forget Frederick Douglass. Jerry and Valerie took us to see his eight-foot bronze statue and monument, dedicated in 1899. In 2018, on the 200th anniversary of his birth, the city placed thirteen statues of Douglass around town. Two have been vandalized. One of those that remains is at the site of Corinthian Hall, where Douglass delivered his most famous oration.

It's sad that the phonograph did not arrive in time to record Frederick Douglass's voice. Yet in the summer following George Floyd's murder, people around the nation held Independence Day readings of Douglass's 1852 Corinthian Hall speech, "What to the Slave is the Fourth of July." One particularly striking version was by four of his young descendants.[68] His words at Corinthian Hall that day can yet inspire both passion and unease:

> For it is not light that is needed, but fire; it is not the gentle shower, but thunder. We need the storm, the whirlwind, and the earthquake. The feeling of the nation must be quickened; the conscience of the nation must be roused; the propriety of the nation must be startled; the hypocrisy

of the nation must be exposed; and its crimes against God and man must be proclaimed and denounced.

What, to the American slave, is your Fourth of July? I answer; a day that reveals to him, more than all other days in the year, the gross injustice and cruelty to which he is the constant victim. To him, your celebration is a sham; your boasted liberty, an unholy license; your national greatness, swelling vanity; your sounds of rejoicing are empty and heartless; your denunciation of tyrants, brass fronted impudence; your shouts of liberty and equality, hollow mockery.

In a coda to the reading, one of the descendants, the teenage Isadore Dharma Douglass Skinner, in dark-rimmed glasses and a plaid shirt, staring directly into the camera, adds:

Somebody once said that pessimism is a tool of white oppression, and I think that's true. I think in many ways, we are still slaves to the notion that it will never get better. But I think that there is hope, and I think that it's important that we celebrate Black joy and Black life and we remember that change is possible, change is probable, and that there's hope.

As the shadows grew long, Jerry and Valerie took us to find the grave of Frederick Douglass. His hillside resting place wasn't hard to locate. It's a monument and headstone with blue inlaid lettering, as grand as Tubman's is modest. Three American flags had been placed there, in advance of the upcoming Fourth of July weekend. The grandeur shouldn't have surprised us. He was the most photographed man of the nineteenth century. In 1895 his casket was carried through

Washington, guarded by 150 Black veterans of the Grand Army of the Republic.[69]

Frederick Douglass grave, Mount Hope Cemetery, Rochester, New York.

There is a symmetry between the two graves and the lives that they represent. Harriet's voice rings as well, though she lacked the education to leave a written legacy of it. Hers speaks in actions, not just in the lives of the people she led to freedom, and their descendants, but also in the love for her family and friends that would take her, over and over again, back into the belly of the beast. Her aura would lead conductors on the secret network to write in hushed letters, "Harriet Tubman is again in these parts."

x. "You've Shook the Lion's Paw" (New York, Ontario)

Harriet Tubman purchased her permanent home in Auburn in 1859, two years before the start of the Civil War. For most of the preceding decade, her home had been in a small town in Ontario. With the passage of the 1850 Fugitive Slave Law, there was nowhere in the United States that was truly safe for those escaping from slavery. She said, "I wouldn't trust Uncle Sam with my people no longer. I brought them all clear to Canada."[70] She, her family, and her friends formed a community centered around a small white church in St. Catharines. Salem Chapel still stands and would be the last destination of this portion of our ride.

Lynn and I still had a ways to travel from Rochester to Buffalo and on to Canada, and Concetta was supporting us for the rest of the ride. We were anticipating an easy, flat ride along the Erie Canalway. Our main obstacle was the same one faced by the builders of the Canal: the ridge known as the Niagara Escarpment. The builders knew that somehow boats would have to "sail uphill" over this ridge to reach Lake Erie. The solution was an engineering marvel of its time: the "Flight of Five," ascending locks blasted into the hillside that would give the town of Lockport its name. In 1825, while touring the country, an aging Marquis de Lafayette, much impressed, said, "The very rocks rend to welcome me." The Canal was completed some months later. Townspeople along the Canal fired cannons in celebration, one after another, rippling from Buffalo to New York City. Here was a young nation flexing its muscle: *We can do big stuff.*

Much of the Lockport Flight of Five is still intact, with an adjoining path to the top. As we stopped at the base, a local woman asked, "You're going to ride up that?" Lynn and I smiled. It was a common experience on tour. Everyone thinks that their local hill is like a pass in the Rockies. From experience, we could both attest that this one wasn't.

We geared down and spun up. Our reward at the crest was a shop with the perfect western New York name: Lake Effect Ice Cream.

That evening Lynn used her expression for what time we would get started in the morning: "Wheels up at 9:00." But in my experience, the blessing for cyclists had always been "Keep the rubber side down" (as in tires). Outside of Lockport, my wheels literally went up. Attempting to maneuver around a stopped service truck on the Canalway, my rear tire fishtailed in soft sand. I bounced off the truck and down a weed-filled embankment. Lynn's video camera caught the whole thing. All in all, a soft if graceless landing.

Down in the weeds: Fall off the Canalway
path near Lockport, New York.

After a quick repair of bike and pride, Lynn and I approached Buffalo and the torrent that is the Niagara River. One particular place in Buffalo called to me, based on a *New Yorker* article titled "The Underground Railroad for Refugees."[71] The article told of a small place in Buffalo where asylum seekers from around the world gather to escape desperate circumstances, paralleling the journeys of 170 years ago. We wandered through the east side of Buffalo to find this place: the Vive Shelter. It's a weathered red brick building, a former Catholic elementary school that's been in operation as a shelter for thirty-five years. Roughly 90 percent of the asylum seekers there are looking for a life in Canada. Vive is in a neighborhood with some of the lowest real estate values in the country.

Lynn watched the bikes, loaded with much of our gear, while I went inside. Alyssa of their legal office took time to talk with me. Her languages included French, Spanish, and Portuguese, as well as English.

"Why Portuguese?" I asked.

"People leaving the DRC [Congo] go to Angola, and they need to speak the language there, Portuguese," she said. "Knowing Portuguese opens the door for a work permit in Brazil. Then they have a horrendous trip through the Amazon, up through Central America to Texas. From Texas they come here. Many just want to rest for a couple of days before going on to Canada. Kind of a global Underground Railroad."

Vive Shelter, Buffalo, New York.

Though we were watchful of our bikes in this "dangerous neigh-borhood" (an opinion based on the article that led us here), it was far more dangerous for the people inside. Border Patrol agents were said to be around the building frequently, and they carry out raids on immigrants in the city. A staff member at Vive said: "I never thought my country would be the one people had to run from."[72] My thoughts returned to the 1850s poster displayed in the basement of the Mother Bethel Church in Philadelphia: "Be It Known That There Are Now Three Slave-Hunters . . ." Border Patrol agents are a far cry from the "Stealers of Men" warned of in the Philadelphia poster. But then and now, both groups enforce the laws of the land.

The modern-day asylum seekers have much to be afraid of. Over the years, Canada has been far more lenient than the United States in accepting asylum claims. But like everywhere, COVID brought changes. Early in the pandemic, Canada began turning back asylum seekers who walk in from the United States outside of official border crossings.[73] Yet the surge in immigration continues. Vive is overflowing. Illegal crossings continue, including many in winter into Canada's prairie provinces, often with disastrous results. Farmers are often fearful of what the spring thaw will reveal.[74]

For those desperate enough, there is yet another option, closer to Vive. A railroad bridge across the roaring Niagara leads to Canada. There is no pedestrian walkway, and cameras monitor the tracks. But it's possible to hop a freight train and stow away between the cars, where you can't see what's ahead. Delta bluesmen and Depression-era hoboes looking for work knew the technique well: they called it "riding the blind." More recently, Afghans and Salvadorans have appeared at the Vive front desk asking for directions to the railroad bridge.

In Harriet Tubman's time, another railroad crossing arched across the Niagara, a wonder of its day. John Roebling, who would later conceive the Brooklyn Bridge, designed the International Suspension Bridge, the first of its type to carry a railroad. And in another first, passengers could take a train directly to Canada. After opening in 1855, it became Harriet Tubman's preferred route for carrying freedom seekers to the Promised Land.

Lithograph of Niagara Falls Suspension Bridge, where
Harriet Tubman and her charges made many crossings.

One whose story was intimately tied to the Niagara Falls Suspension Bridge was Josiah "Joe" Bailey.[75] We last heard of him, in chapter 2.iii, crossing the Market Street Bridge into Wilmington, Delaware, hidden under a load of bricks. A skilled timber foreman back in Maryland, he was so valuable to his enslavers that he had a $1,500 price on his head. As he moved north with Tubman and three other freedom seekers, he saw that even as far as New York City, the poster with a huge reward followed him. Even worse, the poster noted the distinctive scar on his cheek. Bailey was at once terrified and despondent, convinced that he would be captured. He was silent for the entire trip through New York State.

As the train approached the suspension bridge, the excitement was palpable. On the train, Harriet called her passengers over to see Niagara Falls. Joe Bailey remained in his seat, head in his hands. In a few moments, Harriet realized by the rise to the center of the bridge and the descent on the other side that they had crossed into Canada, the land of Queen Victoria. She jumped across to Joe's seat and shook him hard.

"'Joe, you've shook the lion's paw.'" He did not understand what she meant. "Joe, you're free." Joe Bailey broke his silence in emphatic fashion. As he stepped off the train at the Clifton Station, his shouts and singing drew a crowd.[76]

Lynn, Concetta, and I stopped to visit the site of the old bridge, where only the foundations remain. Built just above the site of the bridge is the new Niagara Falls Underground Railroad Heritage Center. Next to the front door is a larger-than-life image of two Black men in dress coats and cravats, arms folded, waiting.

Inside, our guide spun tales of antebellum espionage. In the 1840s and '50s, as today, Niagara Falls was a prominent tourist attraction, and back then the biggest hotel was the Cataract House. Southern enslavers were among the visitors, frequently bringing their entourage. John Morrison, the headwaiter, led the Black staff in serving them. He and his team were also in the clandestine practice of ferrying the enslaved

---

* From a poem by Black abolitionist Joshua McCarter Simpson titled "Away to Canada," which includes the lines
I'm now embarked for yonder shore,
There a man's a man by law;
The iron horse will bear me o'er,
To shake the lion's paw.

across the river to Canada. The hospitality industry indeed. An 1841 letter to the New Orleans *Times-Picayune* warned:

> The proprietors of the "Cataract House" keep in their employ, as servants, a set of *free negroes*, many of whom have wives and relatives in Canada, and they have an organized plan of taking off all slaves that come to their house . . . It behooves all southern people traveling north to avoid the "Cataract House" at the falls of Niagara.[77]

As Lynn and I rode north from Niagara Falls, we'd have our own high iron to cross. The first bridge, still in the United States, was the span across to Grand Island. We rode up in the air, across a narrow, rusty pedestrian walkway with four lanes of traffic at our elbows. We needed all our concentration to avoid hitting the guardrails as the bridge shook. Our next obstacle en route to Canada was a police road-block. It took us a moment to realize what day it was. The cops were detouring us around the local Fourth of July parade.

Once past the parade, our next destination was clear on the horizon: the Lewiston-Queenston Bridge over the Niagara River gorge to Canada. This was the opposite experience from Grand Island. Traffic was at a standstill. Not wanting to dart between cars, we waited in traffic for forty-five minutes on the approach to Canadian customs. As we stood on the asphalt high above the river, Lynn's bike thermometer read 107°F. When we finally reached the booth, the attendant waved us through for free. In New York City, that only happens for hearses. I guess we didn't look too good.

Our tonic was the last 18 miles of gentle riding through Ontario vineyards to journey's end, St. Catharines. We rolled into town and there, across from a bar and next to a used car lot, sat a little white place of worship. Salem Chapel is the oldest Black church in Ontario, predating Harriet Tubman's time. We sat down to rest in a beautiful little garden next to the church, under a bust of Harriet. Lynn had arranged for a reporter from the local paper to meet us there for an interview, and we made the front page of the *St. Catharines Standard* the next morning.

Harriet's route had taken us through the heart of the modern megalopolis, the I-95 corridor, and the heart of America's Industrial Revolution of the nineteenth century, the Erie Canal. Yet in both places, quiet passageways and shelters exist, then as now: a tunnel under the interstate in Delaware, a preserved safe house backing on the New Jersey Turnpike, a modern safe house in Buffalo. And people of goodwill made themselves available to help travelers along the way. One appeared for us in the garden.

Rochelle Bush opened the chapel and led us downstairs to the parish hall. We sat down and she brought us some much-welcomed cold, clear water. Rochelle's ancestors were freedom seekers. In the basement of the church was the descendant wall, from 1838 to today. Many were members of her family. Henry Louis Gates produced a PBS series entitled *The African Americans: Many Rivers to Cross*. He interviewed her during one episode, and she spoke about her people:

> You had to get out of the South, and you were on your own . . . and then, bounty hunters were after you. To run away, you had to be a little bit bent. I didn't even think about it until I was grown. My God. My people did that? That's how we got here?[78]

For a decade, St. Catharines was Harriet Tubman's community. It must have been remarkable for her to be in a place where a Black community existed, where she would walk down the street without being watched, where families did not need to worry about being ripped apart. The constant burden of gauging whom to trust was lifted. Harriet brought her mother and father to this place. Around the corner on North Street once stood the house where she met John Brown, where he called her "General" and tried to recruit her for his Harpers Ferry raid. Thomas Elliott, of the Dover Eight, settled in St. Catharines as Harriet's right-hand man and would marry her niece. Joe Bailey, after rediscovering his voice when he was off the train, lived out his days here.

Rochelle brought us upstairs into the small chapel with its choir loft. Behind the pulpit were flags of Canada, Britain, Ontario, and the United States. Seated in the pews, we were in Harriet Tubman's Promised Land, the place where she came to worship. Yet here, safe in Canada, at the greatest distance from her Maryland family, she felt its strongest attraction. Harriet's grandmother was from the formidable Asante people of West Africa, one of the very last to be colonized. The Asante belief was that ancestors continued to live in a parallel world but could be sought out in times of need.[79] Perhaps this was part of what drew her south once again. A character in Toni Morrison's novel *Beloved* says about the place where she was enslaved:

> It wasn't sweet and it sure wasn't home. But it's where we were. All together. Comes back whether we want it to or not.[80]

Harriet left the comfort of the Salem Chapel pews for one last trip in late 1860. By this time, possibly to her peril, she had gained considerable renown through speaking engagements in abolitionist venues in

New England. When she gathered enough money, she traveled south again, this time to try to bring her sister Rachel and Rachel's two children out.

When she reached the Eastern Shore, she made a devastating discovery. Rachel had died and her children were nowhere to be found. In what was probably a last-minute decision, she brought the Ennals family, with their three children, on the road out of slavery. It may have been her hardest mission. Her network of conductors had degraded considerably under the increased vigilance of the enslavers. She and the Ennals hid on a small island in a swamp in late November snow and freezing rain. Patrols passed by repeatedly. The baby had to be drugged with paregoric to keep her quiet. One day, as they waited, a Quaker man passed by on the shore, apparently talking to himself. Then they realized that he was giving them directions to a nearby barn, where a horse and wagon awaited. Deliverance. Once more Harriet made good on an escape. Her sister and her children were lost, but the Ennals were free.

Harriet came to live in freedom in St. Catharines, and over the time she spent here, she would journey again and again to bring others to this place. Frederick Douglass, eloquent as ever, wrote of her:

> Most that I have done and suffered in the service of our cause has been public, and I have received much encouragement at every step of the way. You, on the other hand, have labored in a private way. I have wrought in the day—you in the night. . . . The midnight sky and the silent stars have been the witnesses of your heroism.[81]

St. Catharines was the place where Harriet Tubman finally came out of the night.

Lynn Salvo, Rochelle Bush, Harriet Tubman, and the author.
Salem Chapel, St. Catharines, Ontario.

3

Freedom Road West: The River, the Blues, and the Borderland

efore I decided to follow Harriet Tubman's route, before the brass collar in the museum in Vandalia, Illinois, that same museum led me on another ride, to a different portion of the Underground Railroad. In 2011, the curator had one more thing to show me as we walked to an exhibit of old agricultural implements. She held up what looked like a flat-bladed axe.

"This is called a froe. It was used for cutting shingles." She handed it to me. "Its owner gave it to his old foreman. He said he wouldn't be needing it anymore since he had just been elected to the state legislature." She pointed to the initials carved into the iron: AL.

I tried to memorize the weight of the head, the feel of the handle, the pattern of the grain on my fingertips, before giving it back. Was it authentic? I had no idea, and it's probably impossible to verify. I know that I believed it to be real, and that an out-of-the-way county

museum would be just the kind of place to come upon Abraham
Lincoln's axe.

As a nineteen-year-old in 1828, Lincoln made the first of his two
trips on a flatboat, following the current 1,300 miles down the Ohio
and Mississippi Rivers, from Indiana to Louisiana. It was an eventful
journey, avoiding the snags and shoals of the rivers and even fighting
off a nighttime hijacking attempt in Louisiana. Lincoln and his partner,
Allen Gentry, sold their cargo of barrel pork in New Orleans, then
stripped the boat to sell the timber. New Orleans in 1828 was the
bustling land of opportunity, the source of great fortunes in cotton
and sugar and slave trading. As a gangly young man, Lincoln watched
the buying and selling of humans and heard the screams of mothers
separated from their children in the sprawling slave markets there.
The echoes would stay with him for a lifetime and alter the course of
a nation's history.

It occurred to me that I could follow Lincoln's route in reverse,
northbound along the Mississippi and Ohio Rivers. While the rivers
carried Lincoln south, Underground Railroad routes often followed
the rivers north. In 2004, the Adventure Cycling Association put out
an Underground Railroad bicycle route from Mississippi to Ontario,
following part of Lincoln's route on the Ohio River. This was also the
part of the country that would become known as the Borderland in
the period before the Civil War, where the Ohio would separate the free
states of Illinois, Indiana, and Ohio from the slave state of Kentucky. It
was then a land of energetic commerce, intrigue, escapes, and captures.

The first of two western cycling routes, shown in heavy dash below,
began in the Deep South, in the Mississippi Delta. Alan Lomax, who
examined Black music for the Library of Congress in the 1930s, called
the Delta "The Land Where the Blues Began." I called this ride Blues
and the Borderland.

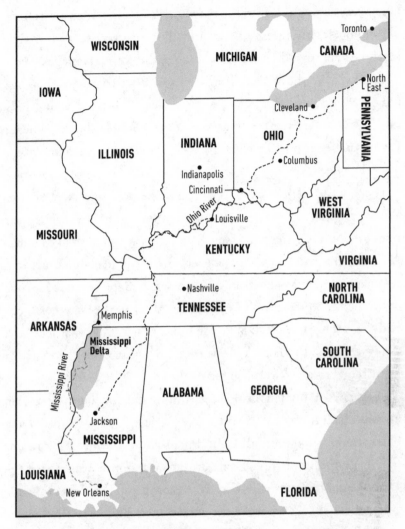

Freedom Road West:
Blues and the Borderland (heavy dash, 1497 miles, 2015);
The River Road (light dash, 556 miles, 2017).

I didn't develop my interest in this route on my own. When I talked about the ride with my friend Rick Sullivan, he immediately noted that I was riding right through the Delta. Rick's a retired psychologist, climate activist, and blues guitarist, with a rich baritone. He's good-looking, with a passing resemblance to actor Tom Skerritt, who played Tom Cruise's wing commander in the movies. Once in Mississippi, a somewhat inebriated young lady said, "Wait—Are you that guy from *Top Gun?*" He shook his head. I later scolded him: "If a cute girl asks if you're a movie star, *tell her you're a movie star.*"

Rick and I first met on an organized bike ride from New York to Washington, in support of the climate movement. Now we do regular rides around DC, and I sit in on Rick's gigs at coffee shops. He has more guitars than bikes. One of them is a shiny steel guitar called a resonator, used in the Delta in the days before amplifiers. He had one of his gigs end prematurely because the owner of the store next door said the resonator was too loud. He has another guitar that folds and can be bungeed to the back of the bike. That guitar was the source of many motel room concerts on the road.

As we began to plan for the ride, I worked on my blues education as well as plotting out the rides day by day. Rick took me to any blues shows he could find, from dinner clubs to diner back rooms to house concerts. I thought about the hard, hot, flat terrain of the Delta, land of cotton fields and the enslaved and the sharecroppers, from whose shacks emerged the great American music. That music is well remembered in Mississippi on the Mississippi Blues Trail, a collection of 210 markers scattered around the state but concentrated in the Delta.

That's how Rick and I came to be unloading bikes and a guitar at Medgar Evers Airport in Jackson, Mississippi, in 2015. Rick rode with me from Jackson through most of Tennessee, but before we headed north on two wheels, we rented a car to hunt down many of the Blues

Trail markers. In the years that followed that first ride, we talked a lot about returning to the Delta. About that time I had been reading about the great 1811 slave revolt along the Mississippi River. So in 2017, a second ride took shape, from New Orleans up the great river along the route of the revolt, ending up in Clarksdale, Mississippi: from the heart of jazz to the heart of the blues. That's the River Road, the ride in light dash above.

In 1828, Lincoln paid his $6 docking fee to tie up his flatboat in New Orleans. Almost two centuries later, Rick and I rolled into Jackson Square to listen for the echoes of what Lincoln heard.

i. The Hidden History of Charles Deslondes (Louisiana)

Rock and roll legend Chuck Berry died the day before Rick and I left for New Orleans. He wrote his famous song "Johnny B. Goode" partly about his great-grandfather, who lived in a cabin in the Louisiana swamps. Berry would have known of the paths that Charles Deslondes walked as he prepared for the greatest slave revolt in American history. In 1811, the swamps and bayous west of New Orleans harbored the maroon camps, ragged hideouts of the formerly enslaved who'd escaped from the brutality of sugar plantations along the Mississippi River. Charles's road took him into these swamps. Unlike the enslaved woman whose face was revealed by Albany archaeologists, we have no image of Charles Deslondes. Based on contemporary accounts, he remains a hazy figure on horseback. Rick and I came to New Orleans to begin our ride north into blues country and to seek out his story.

We started quietly enough on foot in New Orleans, exploring Café du Monde in Jackson Square. It was an old place I frequented forty years earlier, when I came in from stints on oil rigs in the Gulf. The familiar green and white striped awnings frame the tables. Just as in the oil rig days, the chicory smell of steaming mugs of coffee flows out of the kitchen, accompanied by tall trays of fragrant beignets. It took some work to brush the powdered sugar off our pants.

The bright panorama of Jackson Square hides hard stories. Up until 1964, Café du Monde did not serve Black patrons. Earlier still, the fleur-de-lis symbol, ubiquitous in New Orleans, had another meaning. If an enslaved person had escaped for more than a month, the fleur-de-lis would be permanently branded on one shoulder with a hot iron.[1]

Our journey began in earnest a block from the café, on the levee above Jackson Square, in the heart of the French Quarter. The square was bright and busy, the street crowded with tourists and horse carriages. The bronze incarnation of Andrew Jackson tipped his hat from atop a giant horse. We met up with Leon Waters, who runs Hidden History Tours. He was a slight, energetic Black man with an intense aspect, dressed in a pink shirt and tie. His family roots run deep, including a great-great-great maternal grandmother who was enslaved during the 1811 revolt and five relatives who served in the US Colored Troops during the Civil War. Leon's New Orleans is not the Disneyland-for-grownups of Bourbon Street, but the well-washed remnants of the city when it was the country's premier marketplace for the institution of slavery.

"I was nine or ten when my cousin Kizzy, an elderly lady, told me about the revolt," he said. "Her parents had been slaves. She told me that the slaves would take advantage of every opportunity to strike a blow for freedom. She got me interested in the old stories."

Leon led us past the bustle of the square into the narrow streets of the Quarter, to the corner of St. Louis and Chartres Streets. There the present-day Omni Hotel occupies the site of both Hewlett's Exchange and the St. Louis Exchange Hotel, among many places where men, women, and children were bought and sold. He pointed out the fragment of the word "Exchange," still visible on the side of the building.

What had happened to create this sordid industry? In the early nineteenth century, the farmed-out forced labor camps, the tobacco plantations of Maryland, Virginia, and North Carolina, began to decline. At the same time, the expanding use of the newly invented cotton gin gave rise to a new global—and labor-intensive—cash crop. The enslaved of the Upper South were now much more valuable in the expanding cotton fields of Georgia, Alabama, Mississippi, Louisiana, and Texas. Demand for slave labor was virtually unlimited.

Thousands of the enslaved were marched south in chained lines known as coffles. It's a funny word, coffle, so anachronistic and buried in the past that a modern autocorrect will try to change it. One coffle, marching past congressmen on the steps of the US Capitol in the late 1810s, broke into "Hail Columbia," a popular patriotic song of the time.[2] Later coffles were a sight so odious that they had to be rerouted around Washington and away from the Capitol. The rerouting was predictable, since Congress was reluctant to talk about the institution of slavery, much less be exposed to its underside. In 1836, Congress passed a "gag rule," prohibiting discussion of anti-slavery petitions.

The coffles were a part of what has come to be called the Second Middle Passage. From 1790 to 1860, more than one million Black men, women, and children were carried off into the Deep South to feed King Cotton, more than twice the number brought from Africa and a figure that certainly dwarfs the Underground Railroad.[3] It was the largest forced migration in American history, and for many, the destination was New Orleans.

Understanding Leon's walk through the French Quarter requires understanding the context of Charles Deslondes's world in 1811, before the explosion of cotton. Sugar, not cotton, was king then along the Mississippi north of New Orleans. Cane fields were laid out in strips along the river in the region known as the German Coast. For each plantation—that is, forced labor camp—a dock extended from the levee. Multicolumned plantation houses perched on the River Road, dominating the view to the fields behind. The plantations ended at the swamps further inland, the domain of the maroons. White people were vastly outnumbered. In New Orleans in 1811, the ratio of enslaved people and free people of color to whites was three to one. In the outlying parishes, the enslaved made up an even greater proportion.[4]

Much of the sugar plantation culture had been imported from the Caribbean, as had many of the French owners. Cultivating sugar cane was brutally labor intensive. The business model involved large numbers of the enslaved, often worked to death. Something else had been brought from the Caribbean: revolution. In 1791, the enslaved of the French colony of Saint-Domingue, later renamed Haiti, revolted and defeated their overseers. The French sent two massive armies to retake the colony. By 1803, both had been defeated. The following year, Louisiana territorial governor William Claiborne expressed his concern to then secretary of state James Madison that importing more of the enslaved from Saint-Domingue might bring the ideas behind the revolt into Louisiana.[5] But it was too late. The virus of freedom had already been established.

Many contemporary accounts said that Charles Deslondes was born in Saint-Domingue.[6] But according to Leon, there is no documentation revealing where he came into the world. As with most of the enslaved, we know little about him. Leon said:[7]

> Charles would become the principal organizer and leader of the 1811 revolt. He was a laborer on the Andry plantation, up the river from New Orleans, and would embrace the ideals of freedom as inspired by the Haitian Revolution. He would pull together a group or committee of women and men who were the most trustworthy, who were the most dedicated, who were the most determined . . . They would win the majority to the idea of establishing their own independent Black republic where the Africans could rule over or govern themselves. This was their aim—an independent Black republic. They almost succeeded.

Charles must have realized that escape was impossible. They were going to work him to death. If he stayed where he was and kept doing what he was doing, the institution would consume him. So he made what seemed like a suicidal decision: take up arms in a break for freedom, and probably die trying. But Charles's decision was about more than just survival. He sought to establish a new place, a new country along the banks of the great river, forged in desperate revolution. A land of the free and a home of the brave, words that would be put to paper three years later in Baltimore Harbor in 1814.

The revolt that Charles led was well organized but against the odds. The plan was for a coordinated uprising in the plantations along the river, aided by arms from the arsenal in New Orleans. Leon pointed to the corner of Esplanade and Decatur Streets, the site of Fort St. Charles in 1811:

According to their reconnaissance, Fort St. Charles had the largest supply of guns and gunpowder. The authorities issued general orders that stated that 'no Negro can be on the street after 6:00 P.M.' The advanced detachment of former enslaved drew attention in their attempt to capture Fort St. Charles. The authorities observed them after 6:00 P.M. As a result, Gilbert and his detachment of rebels were arrested and brought to Ft. Ferdinand, where they were interrogated (tortured). They did not give up any information.

By the time our tour ended, Leon was fully engaged, his shirtsleeves rolled up as we stopped on the steps of the state supreme court. We sat next to a giant statue of Edward Douglas White, who became chief justice of the US Supreme Court. White was instrumental in the infamous 1896 *Plessy v. Ferguson* decision, codifying racial segregation as "separate but equal" and providing the legal underpinnings of the Jim Crow laws. Homer Plessy was a Black New Orleans shoemaker arrested for boarding a whites-only railcar. He was pardoned by the governor in 2022, but the Supreme Court's ruling against him would stand as the basis for segregation for fifty-eight years. Leon observed the statue with a wry smile.

We had a demonstration here a little while back. The protesters climbed up on the White statue and put a KKK hood on his face and a sign on his chest that read: "This is what a terrorist looks like." Police had a heck of a time getting it down.

Leon was being modest. He is one of the elders of Take 'Em Down NOLA, a group led by young Black activists to remove monuments and names of streets and schools dedicated to white supremacists.[8] Their work would shortly bear fruit.

I turned the conversation back to 1811. "Seems like we have lots of memorials around to Americans fighting for their freedom, but none to enslaved Americans."

Leon corrected me. "They weren't Americans. And their children wouldn't be Americans until after the Civil War."

Leon could be prickly, impatient with tourists like us as he explained his story with detail and passion. He needed to get across that the 1811 slave revolt wasn't some ignorant, bloodthirsty mob coming down the River Road. Charles's army was a well-planned but desperate reach for freedom, a revolution that would be put down only with a storm of iron flying through the air.

We set out the next day to find a little piece of that history. Charles's road would take us forty-seven miles up the river. The rebels had tried to reach New Orleans; we would ride to where they had started. On the way out of town, the massive post–Reconstruction era statue of Robert E. Lee loomed. It was dedicated the same year (1884) that the Statue of Liberty was presented to the United States ambassador.[9] In the months before our ride, Take 'Em Down NOLA had events at the Lee statue. Two months after we rode by, cranes would come to take it, along with three others, to a warehouse. The statue of Justice Edward Douglas was moved to the Supreme Court Museum inside the building in 2020. In describing why the statues were taken down, the mayor of New Orleans, Mitch Landrieu, said of them, "They were erected purposefully to send a strong message to all who walked in their shadows about who was in charge in this city."[10]

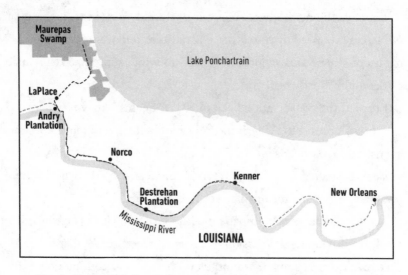

Charles Deslondes's Road. (heavy dash: Route of the 1811 slave revolt); (light dash: The 2017 bike route from New Orleans).

It was already hot up on the levee even in March, with a stiff wind blowing out of the Gulf. The great river rumbled to our left, draining the center of the continent all the way from the northern Rockies. A steady stream of giant ships passed us, with the sound of thundering engines and water surging off the bows. The commerce of much of the middle of the nation was moving by. It didn't take long to catch a whiff of the refineries. The eighty-five miles between New Orleans and Baton Rouge have 150 petrochemical plants. The span is popularly known as Cancer Alley, disproportionately poor and Black. Many are the descendants of the enslaved who worked in the cane fields by the river.

When we stopped for lunch, we asked the waitress for a couple of glasses of water.

"Nope," she said. "Bring you a bottle of water if you want. Tap water's no good." Taking the hint, Rick refilled our bike jugs with bottled water. When we stopped for coffee later across from a refinery,

I mentioned to Rick that they must use bottled water for the coffee. He was suspicious. Then I gave him a line that heavy metals are adsorbed to particulates, and that water coming through a coffee filter was probably fine. Just when I thought he was buying it, I noticed he didn't finish his coffee. I didn't finish mine, either.

I first heard the rebels' footsteps in Kenner. Today a steady roar of jets comes from the nearby airport, some twenty miles from New Orleans by the winding River Road. But on a rainy night two hundred years ago, an army of the newly free came to rest here, listening in the darkness for approaching forces that they must have known were coming.

The slave revolt launched on January 8, 1811, just after sundown. In a coordinated action, the rebels swept out of the Maurepas Swamp, hideout of the runaways, and through the Andry Plantation in Laplace, where Charles Deslondes was enslaved.[11] Charles led the vanguard on horseback down the river toward New Orleans, gathering recruits and swelling the army to over five hundred. By the end of the next day, they had created, however briefly, a 30-mile liberated zone. They stopped for the night at the Fortier Plantation in Kenner, where we stood. They planned to march on New Orleans the next day.

But the authorities in New Orleans had been busy. Alerted by the attack on Fort St. Charles and by enslavers streaming into the city, a force of about four hundred well-armed regular army and planters' militia moved up the river to meet the approaching rebels. They arrived near the rebel encampment at about 4:00 A.M. on January 10th. With few firearms, the rebels made a brief attack but then retreated up the river to the Bernoudy Plantation, in what is now Norco.

Rick and I rode up the river toward Norco, on the path of the retreating footsteps. Some of the plantation houses still exist along the road, though not Bernoudy. We passed Destrehan, amazingly a destination for parties and weddings, with tall columns in front in the classic Greek Revival style. Plantation tourism remains a significant part of the travel industry here, in places that Imani Perry describes as "sites of death and rape, violence and theft—of children, names, life, and personal autonomy."[12] Destrehan itself was the site, along with many others, of the tribunals and executions that would follow the events of early January 1811.

Bike path on the levee at the Shell Refinery, Norco, Louisiana, the place where the planters' militia caught up with the rebel army.

White plumes came off the cracking towers as we approached the giant refinery at Norco, the site where the army caught up to the rebels. Light artillery and muskets opened up against the poorly armed insurgents. A massacre resulted. Perhaps thirty to sixty died on the spot. Many of the rebels fled into the nearby Maurepas Swamp, where troops pursued them over the next several days.

Governor Claiborne decreed that punishment for the rebels should have "a goal of making a terrible example" for all in the future who might try to win their freedom by force of arms. Charles Deslondes was captured in the Maurepas Swamp on the evening of January 11th and brought to Andry Plantation. Enough white landowners were present for a "court," and Charles was convicted, tortured, and executed the next day.[13] His head, like dozens of others, was placed on a pike along the road. They lined the river for fifty miles to New Orleans. Joseph Conrad wrote a story about heads on posts along the Congo River. The Congo seems a distant place, but America has had its own heart of darkness.

When we visited, Andry Plantation had fallen on hard times. It lay abandoned, not far from the River Road in LaPlace. No one had lived there for at least a decade. A sapling grew through the wooden front porch steps. Near where we stayed in LaPlace, air boats take guests on guided tours of the Maurepas Swamp Wildlife Management Area. There's a lot more water than in Charles's day, as southern Louisiana has one of the highest rates of sea level rise in North America.

Things change. History is both reborn and reflected upon itself. Andry Plantation, where Charles Deslondes was enslaved, has been refurbished and reopened as the 1811/Kid Ory Historic House, named both for the revolt and for one of the pioneers in New Orleans jazz. Sadly, the 1811/Kid Ory House closed in 2022. Across the river, Whitney Plantation centers its exhibits on the life of the enslaved, including a rendering of those lost in the Deslondes revolt.

Andry Plantation in 2017, in disrepair, but more recently refurbished.

In 2019, an artist by the name of Dread Scott organized a march of reenactors, in 1811 period costumes, out of the Andry house and along the route of the revolt, our bicycle route. This time the march didn't stop at Kenner but made it all the way to New Orleans. In their wake, they left kiosks explaining the revolts at Andry and Destrehan, new examples of Toni Morrison's benches by the road.[14]

The time of the Deslondes revolt casts a shadow on today. Iris Carter is a Black woman profiled in the documentary *Women of Cancer Alley*. She lived with her family at Norco, the place where the rebels were trapped. She had "roots going back 200 years, to the time of the slave revolt." But after years living there between two refineries and losing her mother to a mysterious disease, Carter left her ancestral home when it was bought out by Shell Oil.[15]

Norco is on the predominantly Black eastern bank of the Mississippi, south of Baton Rouge. It's likely not coincidental that this is where the highest concentration of petrochemical plants are sited. The reasons all the plants are located here are straightforward: Land is cheap and there's access to transport on the river. There's one more reason, the same reason that the Dakota Access Pipeline was run next to North Dakota's Standing Rock Reservation and not on the more direct route through the white communities of Bismarck: a poor community of color, with less political power, is less likely to resist. Places like Standing Rock and this stretch of the Mississippi have become ground zero for the environmental justice movement. Civil rights leader Rev. Dr. William Barber describes this part of the Mississippi River: "The same land that held people captive through slavery is now holding people captive through this environmental injustice and devastation."[16]

Sharon Lavigne is a retired Black special education teacher from St. James Parish, just up the river from the site of the slave revolt, and also the place where a young Abraham Lincoln was attacked on his flatboat. Lavigne learned in 2018 that the Formosa Petrochemical Corporation was proposing to build a massive new plant for plastic feedstocks within a mile and a half of her house.[17] She and several of her neighbors formed Rise St. James as an organization to resist the new chemical plants. She had her own experience with a nearby plant.

Something was familiar about this part of the river. When I worked on a ship, I was a diver, sometimes going out on winter dives in marginal weather. It was my job, but my stomach would get in a knot at the idea of rolling off a small boat into the stone-cold ocean. It was a time when fear felt like the black neoprene rubber of our wet suits.

Sharon Lavigne.

Sharon Lavigne had other reasons for fear. Just down the river from St. James is the only place in the United States where neoprene is made, the Denka Performance Elastomer plant. We had ridden right by it. The plant releases chloroprene, the principal component of neoprene and a chemical so toxic the Environmental Protection Agency says nearby residents face the highest risk in the country of developing cancer from air toxins.[18] High levels of chloroprene are in the neighborhoods around the Denka plant, and a peer-reviewed study found that the prevalence of cancer and other illness correlated with proximity to the plant.[19]

Sharon Lavigne's group had some success. Rise St. James managed to halt construction of a proposed chemical plant two miles from St. James. "They let these companies come into our Black and brown neighborhoods when they know this stuff is killing us," Lavigne said. "This would have been two miles downwind from my house. I wasn't going to allow any more industry into St. James parish."[20]

The issues on this stretch of the Mississippi have attracted national attention. In one of his earliest executive order announcements, President Biden stated that "environmental justice will be at the center of all we do, addressing the disproportionate health and environmental and economic impacts on communities of color—so-called fenceline communities—especially . . . the hard-hit areas like Cancer Alley in Louisiana or the Route 9 corridor in the state of Delaware." Sen. Bill Cassidy of Louisiana denounced the use of "Cancer Alley" as a "slam on our state," putting the blame for higher cancer rates on lifestyle choices like smoking and overeating.[21]

Rise St. James is still fighting the proposed Formosa plant, and the high-level attention can't hurt. A Louisiana judge canceled the plant's air permits in September 2022, writing that "the blood, sweat, and tears of their ancestors is tied to the land."[22] In the meantime, Sharon Lavigne won the international Goldman Environmental Prize for her efforts to keep new chemical plants out of her already polluted community.

The battles of two hundred years ago don't seem so distant here. On a patch of grass next to a turning lane on a busy highway, not far from the banks of the Mississippi, we found an old brass historical marker mentioning in passing the largest slave revolt in North America:

WOODLAND PLANTATION

ACQUIRED IN 1793 & 1808 BY MANUEL ANDRY,

A COMMANDANT OF THE GERMAN COAST.

MAJOR 1811 SLAVE UPRISING ORGANIZED HERE.

ORY BROS. AND A. LASSEIGNE WERE LAST OWNERS OF

PLANTATION.

The busy highway is US Route 61, running up the Mississippi from New Orleans to Minnesota. The road is known as the Blues Highway.

Rick and I would follow it north. Leon's tour had touched on unknown history for us. We talked through what we had learned over a beer later. We were a couple of white guys who'd done a little reading and were surprised at what we'd found. But for Leon, the history was never hidden. His was an oral history, passed from the enslaved to Black Union soldiers to sharecroppers to him. It was always alive and remains so today.

ii. The Blues Storm (Mississippi)

Riding north to the Mississippi Delta on the Blues Highway seemed to be a way to get close to the people of the Underground Railroad. This land was the destination for many of the people sold into bondage in New Orleans. The cotton fields of the Delta and the enslaved who tended them generated much of the wealth of ante-bellum America. After the Civil War, the institution of slavery gave way to the institution of sharecropping. Out in the shimmering heat, the field hollers, the call-and-response songs, the spirituals, and the distant rhythms of West Africa slowly came together to birth the blues, the quintessential American music. This place, the Delta, would also become the wellspring of the Great Migration, as African Americans moved north and west to reshape every American city in the early-mid twentieth century. In my mind, the arc of history from the slave ships to the Great Migration is all of a piece, and the blues are its soundtrack.

Clarksdale, Mississippi, is the Promised Land, the heart of the blues. Tucked into the back of the Clarksdale's Delta Blues Museum is their prized exhibit, the lovingly restored wooden sharecropper cabin of McKinley Morganfield. Back in the summer of 1941, a man from the Library of Congress set up recording equipment in this cabin to capture Morganfield playing the blues. The music world would know him as Muddy Waters. Rick and I had come to find his road.

As we were leaving the museum at noon, we asked the man at the desk if he knew of any music in town for the afternoon. There was a little twinkle in his eye. "Well, it just so happens . . ." He got out from behind the counter and took us to his car. A black guitar case and amp emerged from the trunk.

"Follow me." Daddy Rich gave us a little motion with his head. The pied piper led us down a back alley, dodging puddles from the last night's rain, to a sidewalk stage a few blocks away. He set up his amp, put on his shades, and lit up Yazoo Avenue for the next hour. Clarksdale's like that. It's a little beat down, with every other storefront abandoned. But the blues live on here.

Our pilgrimage toward Clarksdale rolled up the Mississippi River through Baton Rouge, northbound on Highway 61. Musicians know all about the Blues Highway. One of Bob Dylan's early albums is *Highway 61 Revisited*. The road passes all the way from New Orleans through the Delta clear up to Dylan's hometown in Minnesota. But the poetry was a little lacking on the stretch north out of Baton Rouge. A thick, rancid chemical smell hung in the air. The busy four-lane road with no shoulders rolls past the massive ExxonMobil refinery through an expanse of gas stations, scrap metal shops, and liquor stores. It's called the Scenic Highway. After we pulled into a vacant lot to check on directions, a pickup truck did a U-turn and pulled up next to us. The (white) driver leaned out the window.

"You boys don't belong here. You know how many murders happen in this neighborhood? Best get on down the road."

It struck me later that this was an example, as Clint Smith's book title would put it, of "how the word is passed." It reminded me of an encounter some years earlier, at a diner in Rapid City, South Dakota. I mentioned to the waitress that my friend and I were going to cycle through the Pine Ridge (Lakota/Sioux) Reservation—then, as now, one of the poorest places in the United States. She said, "It's like Harlem. Worse than Harlem." I was pretty sure she hadn't been to either place.

After a few more miles, the country started to open up. Our route turned away from the river and into the piney woods of Louisiana and southern Mississippi. We couldn't have followed the river anyway. A giant bend is taken up by the Louisiana State Penitentiary at Angola. The prison was built on an old plantation, once the property of Isaac Franklin. His Alexandria, Virginia, firm, Franklin and Armfield, was once the largest slave trading operation in the country. Later in its history, Angola's private owner leased the prisoners' labor for profit. It's some measure of the prison's ominous reputation that a guard tower from Angola resides in the National Museum of African American History and Culture in Washington. The legacy remains. Louisiana has the highest rate of incarceration in the world. The prison system is 66 percent Black, twice the percentage of Black people in the state.[23]

The inland route carried its own excitement. A violent squall line passed over our hotel at dawn. But the radar looked clear after breakfast, so we decided to make for the state line, into a dark, hilly forest full of logging trucks. On a long stretch of scrub pine, a sign appeared: MISSISSIPPI. BIRTHPLACE OF AMERICA'S MUSIC. I remember thinking: *We must be going the right way.*

Passing through Centreville, we saw grass growing through cracks in the parking lot of the abandoned hospital. For the whole morning, the weather sniffed around behind us. We could look back and see an ominous sky to the south: dark scalloped clouds, perfectly shaped. A minivan pulled up next to us on the road. The woman behind the wheel rolled down the window.

"Y'all know there's a tornado warning up? You can get shelter at the church back in town."

I waved thanks and we pulled over. The cell signal was good enough to pick up a Doppler radar.

"That nasty stuff should be scooting by to the south," I said. "If we keep heading north, we'll ride out of it."

Rick looked skeptical but thought better of going back into the boiling skies. We put on a serious pace northbound, making our way into clearer weather and deeper forest. We emerged fifty miles later in Natchez. The next two days would take us to Vicksburg, the southern edge of the Mississippi Delta.

The Delta's different from the rest of the South, or anywhere else for that matter. It's actually the delta of the Yazoo River, where it flows into the Mississippi. The hot, flat, fertile land is perfect for cotton. It attracted the massive forced labor camps that became known as plantations when it was first cleared in the early nineteenth century. Not so much changed after the Civil War. The vast plantations shifted to the sharecropper system, and the plantations became small towns unto themselves, some even with their own printed money.

The Delta has thick, muddy soil that clings to your shoes. Harvesting cotton from it was a brutal life. Within the flavors of the Delta blues lives a hard-edged expression of a hard place, with echoes of the call-and-response of field gangs. From that grueling life came an authentic American music that reverberates around the world.

Rick and I came looking for one place in particular. Rick had been telling me about Dockery for years. Dockery Farms, four miles west of

Ruleville, is on a lonely two-lane, marked on the road by a preserved 1930s-era gas station. Will Dockery, the 1895 founder, had no particular interest in music. He even frowned on his son's interest in piano lessons.[24] But out behind the big house was something different. The concerts would start on Saturday afternoons on the front porch of the commissary and later move across a one-lane bridge to a cleared-out sharecropper shack known as the Frolickin' House. Will Dockery and his son Joe, who inherited the place, never thought all that much about what was going on out back. The garden wasn't tended, but it was allowed to grow.

Many of the biggest names in the blues lived or came of age at Dockery: Willie Brown, Son House, Howlin' Wolf, Pops Staples. Blues legend Robert Johnson played there in what were sometimes all-night performances. But the man most associated with Dockery was a field hand by the name of Charley Patton. In his heyday in the '20s and early '30s, he was a flamboyant musician who would play guitar with his teeth and behind his head. He was one of the most important early Delta bluesmen. His early recordings on vinyl survive. One of his songs would come to me as out of a dream.

Rick and I walked from the road onto the grass on a pure, quiet Saturday, past the giant cotton gin and the restored front porch of the commissary, now an outdoor concert venue. Just beyond the porch was a marker of the Mississippi Blues Trail, titled "Birthplace of the Blues?" Under the marker was a console with a single unmarked red button. I pushed it.

Speakers from every building erupted with a scratchy recording of Charley Patton, "Spoonful Blues." Rick looked over at me: "Did you do that?" I held up my hands in my best "Who, me?" We padded through the grass between the buildings as the primal blues from almost a hundred years ago wafted through the Delta morning.

Listening to Charley Patton.

We stopped for lunch in Ruleville, by the statue of a woman with her arm up, speaking in full throat into a microphone. On the statue's base: "I am sick and tired of being sick and tired." This is the gravesite of Fannie Lou Hamer, civil rights activist. When she tried to register to vote in 1962, she was fired from her job at the plantation the next day. The next year she was severely beaten in jail but still became one of the first African Americans to register to vote in Sunflower County. In 1964 she led the Mississippi Freedom Democratic Party delegation to the Democratic Convention in Atlantic City, in opposition to the all-white seated delegation. Hers was one of the prominent voices behind passage of the 1965 Voting Rights Act.

Rick and I rode the back way north to Clarksdale on the New Africa Road. Even in early April, the heat shimmered off the fields. The route was only forty miles and flat, but we were cutting a swath through the heavy air. We kept pouring water down our throats, but it was never enough. We stopped at the only bit of shade, under the awning of an abandoned gas station. I sat with my back to the wall, the dirt of the parking lot stuck to the sweat on my hands. Out in the distance was Parchman.

Parchman Farm was, and is, the Mississippi state prison. You think you've never been there, but it's been in your mind's eye: think *Cool Hand Luke* and *Oh Brother, Where Art Thou?*—striped uniforms and bags of cotton. Much like Angola, Parchman was a center for convict labor. In the early twentieth century, Parchman's convicts were second only to income tax as the largest source of revenue for the state of Mississippi.[25] Along with true criminals, court records demonstrate the capture and imprisonment of thousands of random indigent citizens, many for violations of laws written to intimidate African Americans, like vagrancy or riding freight cars without a ticket.[26]

In 1961, Parchman was also seen by the governor as the solution to an out-of-state problem. The Freedom Riders, interracial waves of young civil rights activists, had resolved to ride then-segregated buses into the heart of the South. Beatings and bus burnings failed to stem the tide. So they were arrested by the hundreds and sent to the hardest prison in the state. Today the mug shots of Freedom Riders at Parchman form something of an honor roll of the Civil Rights Movement. They include the face of a young John Lewis.

At the Fannie Lou Hamer statue, Rick and I met a nurse who worked at Parchman. She could only shake her head about the situation there. In 2022, the US Justice Department released a report on Parchman that described how conditions, including a lack of mental health services and an overreliance on solitary confinement, contributed to a spate of deadly violence among inmates. A 2019 riot there went on for weeks.[27] Imani Perry writes, "Yes, slavery was abolished, Jim Crow is over, but the prisons, the persistence of poverty, are constant reminders of how the past made the present."[28]

Outside Parchman is a marker on the Mississippi Blues Trail. In its way, Parchman was the birthplace of the blues as much as Dockery. Some of the greatest blues performers did time under the gaze of guards in those fields. Son House, a former Parchman inmate, sang, in "Mississippi County Farm Blues":

> Wish I was a baby in my mama's arms,
> Wouldn't-a been here working on the County Farm.
> I'd rather be broke, lord, and out of doors,
> Than to be here working on the police roll.

Looking through the heat from our perch at the old gas station, Rick spoke of seeing Son House play many years ago. "It was an incredible concert, but you could hear how much pain was coming through and how much vulnerability he was showing. He was out on the edge. When he played his blues, he took you along for the ride."

In an earlier time, back in the '30s and '40s, Alan Lomax of the Library of Congress wandered the Delta in search of the blues. He found fertile ground at Parchman. One recording of his, of inmates chopping timber, was released as part of an album titled *Murderers' Home* and was studied by a new generation of British musicians in the late 1950s. But his most famous recording was made in 1941, when he traveled south with John Work of Fisk University to Clarksdale to record one of Son House's students: Muddy Waters. Rick and I packed up from our little square of shade behind Parchman and followed the road to Clarksdale as well.

The evening after Daddy Rich's sidewalk concert, we arrived at Clarksdale's biggest venue, the Ground Zero Blues Club, co-owned by Clarksdale native Morgan Freeman. The painted brick facade is peeling, and the front doors are covered in graffiti. Bolted to the porch is the bench seat of a van. Scrawled on the back in magic marker is BABY DON'T BREAK YOUR MAMA'S HEART. Inside is a sprawling, spartan music hall, with wait staff hauling out barbecue and beer against the backdrop of a dozen guitars on the wall. We settled in for an evening of bluesmen trading riffs across the stage.

The next day brought us to the furrows of a newly planted field just north of Clarksdale. The sharecropper shack in the Delta Blues Museum once stood here, on the grounds of the Stovall Plantation. Muddy Waters must have looked with some wariness at Lomax and Work's car driving up the dirt road that day in August 1941. He'd never heard of the Library of Congress, and he suspected that his visitors might be revenuers interested in his whiskey business. After introducing themselves, Lomax and Work pulled their bulky recording equipment out of the trunk. Waters reached for his guitar.

Today a few strokes on a keyboard can produce excerpts from that fateful recording session, together with Lomax's interview after the song was complete. Lomax and Work had found a link in the "royal lineage of America's great guitar players,"[29] from Charley Patton at

Dockery to Son House to the shack at Stovall. There was magic for Waters as well. When they played the recording back, Waters heard himself sing for the first time.

Muddy Waters left the Delta for Chicago two years later, part of the Great Migration out of the South. The worlds of Chicago and Mississippi became intertwined. The Illinois Central Railroad up the great river valley was known as "the chicken bone express," for the pasteboard boxes lovingly packed with food from back home for the Delta pilgrims.[30]

The journey to Chicago led Waters to sign with Chess Records, the vanguard of a cultural explosion along with Howlin' Wolf, Etta James, Chuck Berry, and Ike Turner. Waters went from the acoustic guitar of Stovall to the electric guitar of the emerging Chicago blues. Muddy Waters burst on the music scene of the late '40s and '50s in a way that was all but invisible to white America. But others were listening. When Keith Richards ran into his childhood friend Mick Jagger on a train in 1961, Jagger had a Muddy Waters album. They spent the rest of the day listening to it, and their band would get its name from the title of one of Waters's songs. As Waters would say later, "The blues had a baby and they named it rock 'n' roll." It all started in the shack at Stovall. Or perhaps at Parchman or Dockery before that.

Rick and I wandered back to Clarksdale for one last night. The Ground Zero is a great place, but we were looking for one of the old-time juke joints we'd heard about. Everyone pointed us to Red's. As it's sitting across the street from a graveyard, you can be forgiven for thinking it's another of Clarksdale's abandoned storefronts. The metal awning is tattered, and plywood covers the windows. The night we came in, tornado warnings were up again in nearby Arkansas.

We made it in as the rain started whipping across the pavement and into the streetlights. Red's is just barely there. A bar, some chairs on an uneven floor, a drum set across the room. Neon red lights in the shape of notes on the wall. There's indoor plumbing, but not by much. The bathroom leans at an angle, and you get the sense that it just might tumble off into the river behind. Up on the wall is Red's slogan: BACKED BY THE RIVER. FRONTED BY THE GRAVE.

Bilbo Walker was the bluesman for the night. Black suit, wide pin-stripes. He's about eighty and muttering: "This is not my night. This is not going to be my night." His bass player was stuck across the river with the tornadoes.

Bilbo settled up to the mic. "Ain't got no full band. Still gonna entertain ya."

Robert Johnson, "Kind Hearted Woman," "Dust My Broom." Muddy Waters, "Got My Mojo Workin." Chuck Berry, "Johnny B. Goode." Incredibly, Bilbo was playing bass lines along with the lead. He kicked the tip bucket out into the floor.

"I'm workin' twice as hard up here. Y'all need to help out." The crowd stepped up, reverently, one by one.

At the end of the first set, a long-haired white guy stepped up and mumbled something into Bilbo's ear. Bilbo's brow furrowed. He produced a second, gleaming white, guitar and handed it to him. The blues fired up again, and now there was a strong bass guitar. Bilbo's lead soared. The building was shaking, either from the blues inside or the tempest outside. Bilbo's mood changed, and his face lit up.

"Now that's back up," Bilbo said. "Where you from, son?"

"Helena, Arkansas."

Later Bilbo sat out, and the bassman took over for a while. "If I'd known this would happen, I would have brought my set list. I'm honored to be playing here at Red's."

Sometime after midnight the crowd dispersed into the driving rain. The blues storm was over, and Red's stood for one more night.

Bilbo Walker.

iii. Return to Avalon (Mississippi)

Avalon, my hometown, always on my mind
Pretty mamas in Avalon, want me there all the time
New York's a good town, but it's not for mine
Goin' back to Avalon, where I have a pretty mama all the time
　　　　　—Mississippi John Hurt, "Avalon Blues"

We had one more bluesman yet to find, one more piece in our Delta quilt. Rick did a pretty good job of dragging me around the blues country, covering much of the territory in a rental car. We set off on the Mississippi Blues Trail, that series of roadside markers honoring one of the heartlands of American music. We saw countless blues sites, from a lonely panel for Skip James on an overgrown shoulder to a full-fledged museum for B. B. King. But Rick, still on his quest, was resolved to track down an old favorite of his. Rick's gray-bearded, ponytailed teacher and blues master, Scott Ainslie, had given us a lead. Scott told us that, out of the hot, flat Mississippi Delta, up in the Loess Hills, there was a museum for Mississippi John Hurt, open by appointment. When we reached Jackson, Rick called the number that Scott had given him and spoke to a man named Floyd. He said to meet him at Avalon at 1:00. It all sounded a little sketchy.

The biggest town near Avalon is Greenwood. Dusty rows of brick buildings, many vacant, lined the streets. The Delta's like that: the life, the richness, is behind the facade. A 1950s vintage sign hung outside the Crystal Grill: AIR CONDITIONED. Inside was a bustling oasis, nearly full. A cooler of homemade pies graced the entrance. On the wall, a T-shirt with crossed guitars read: DELTA BLUES TRAIL. IT'S THE RHYTHM IN OUR SOULS THAT KEEPS US ALIVE. We weren't the first on this road.

We fortified ourselves for the ride to Avalon with a bowl of home-made gumbo. The gravel in the parking lot crackled under our tires as we turned north, John Hurt playing out of the car speakers. Avalon was the legendary island where King Arthur was taken to heal his wounds, so perhaps I was expecting something a little mystical. But Avalon on the GPS, well, wasn't. We followed the voice of the nice iPhone lady. Mysticism gave way to barrenness. The place where Avalon was supposed to be featured falling-down buildings with grass growing up through the porches in front of soybean fields. But maybe we weren't completely lost. A Blues Trail marker to Mississippi John Hurt stood by the roadside. It was 1:00. We waited.

In 1928, at the height of the Jazz Age, Okeh Records in New York was scouring the South for new sounds. They sent their engineer, Bob Stevens, on a trip down to the Delta to look for "race music," then back north through the Loess Hill country for "hillbilly music."[31] As he wandered from one small-town club to the next, he noted that "we kept hearing about some wild blues singer named John Hurt."

It took some tracking, but Stevens finally knocked on the door at Hurt's house in Avalon. Hurt invited him in, threw some logs on the fire, and began to play. Stevens was enchanted. John Hurt was soon on the way to Memphis to make his first recordings. Somewhere in the process, Okeh added the prefix "Mississippi" to his name.

John Hurt played a different kind of blues, closer to what we might call folk music. His songs are intricate and funny and wise, with delicate, inventive finger picking. In film close-ups that still survive, we see bony, calloused fingers dancing across guitar strings. He was a warm man, and it came through in his music.

It was fundamentally different from the hard Delta blues of artists like Charley Patton or Son House. Sometimes their blues verge on the apocalyptic, with titles like "Levee Camp Moan" and "John the Revelator," and lyrics like *Every day seem like murder here.*" The land of Parchman Prison and sharecropper shacks found its way into their songs. John Hurt's music isn't that way. Wry, sometimes bawdy, but never apocalyptic. The warmth was genuine, but it was also likely a way to keep the brutal racism of the Delta at bay.

After John Hurt came back to Avalon, a record arrived for him in the mail. But he had no record player. So he went to the house of the white woman whose cattle he was tending, and she cranked up her Victrola. Hurt waited outside behind the screen door and heard the sound of his voice coming out of the great brass horn. "Oh that's you in that song," the woman exclaimed.[32]

Soon Hurt was back on the train, this time to New York, where he did more recordings for Okeh. He struck up a friendship with the janitor in the building, and he stayed with him for a week in

December 1928. Sometime during that week, homesick in New York, he wrote "Avalon Blues." At thirty-five, his prospects as a recording artist were bright. Back in Mississippi, he wrote multiple letters to Okeh, looking for the next studio session, the next gig. It was the cusp of the Great Depression. He waited.

There's not much traffic on Mississippi Route 7 past Avalon. Rick and I walked around the abandoned buildings, waiting for something to happen. We weren't expecting theater. We squinted up the arrow-straight road to where the sky faded from blue to pale white and the road turned to a shimmering lake. Slowly, out of the sun, a battered pickup appeared, floating on the asphalt. It had rounded fenders and bug-eye headlights, with no paint left on the hood. The pickup slowed as it approached us. A Black man with salt-and-pepper hair and the hint of a smile was at the wheel. He looked us up and down but didn't stop. Wordlessly, he leaned out the window and motioned with his arm to follow. Rick and I looked at each other and shrugged. Soon we were roaring up a winding dirt road out of the flats of the Delta and into the hills and the piney woods. Sometimes we lost the truck and were only following the dust trail.

The pickup finally pulled up to a tottering building with creepers growing up the side. The faded Coca-Cola sign said VALLEY STORE. The man behind the wheel stepped out into the knee-deep grass. He wore a John Deere shirt and camouflage pants. Floyd Bailey introduced himself as the caretaker of the Mississippi John Hurt Museum, just up the road.

"Not too many folks left around Avalon these days. But right here on this porch is where John Hurt used to play."

The call from Okeh never came for John Hurt. In 1929, the Great Depression devastated the record business, along with most others. In nearby Greenwood, five out of six banks closed.[33] If Hurt was disappointed, there's no record of it. He scratched out a living like most men in the hills, doing odd jobs from tending cattle to factory work to cutting railroad ties. He continued to perform at local juke joints and family gatherings. Photographs from the 1950s show Hurt playing at the Valley Store. About this time, he was teaching his son to play. He told him it was like riding a bicycle: "Once you learn it, you never forget it."[34]

The year 1963 changed John Hurt's life completely. It was both a miraculous year for him and a terrifying one for African Americans in Mississippi. Medgar Evers, the NAACP field director in Mississippi, would be assassinated a hundred miles away in Jackson. Martin Luther King wrote his "Letter from Birmingham Jail." The following year, the Klan burned sixty-one crosses in a single night across Mississippi then torched twenty Black churches during the course of the year. John Hurt said little, publicly or privately. Like most people caught in war zones, he did his best to keep his head down.

Music was changing dramatically as well. With the blossoming of folk and rock 'n' roll, white musicians were fanning out, searching for the authentic source of their music. Mick Jagger and Keith Richards studied Muddy Waters riffs in England. Al Wilson, who would go on to fame with Canned Heat at Woodstock, tracked down Son House and his primal blues in Central New York.

On the folk music scene, the dusty 78s from the 1920s were treasures sought after by collectors. Mississippi John Hurt's music became a staple in Greenwich Village, New York, coffee shops. His recordings had survived, but no one knew if he had. A collector by the name of Dick Spottswood found an old Okeh record, with a clue in the lyrics: "Avalon's my hometown, always on my mind." In the road atlas then, just like on Google Maps today, Avalon could still be found. He asked his colleague, Tom Hoskins, to stop by Avalon on his way to Mardi Gras in 1963.

Hoskins approached a man at the Valley Store, asking where he could find John Hurt's gravesite. The man answered, "If he ain't died since, he went that way with two sacks of groceries at eleven o'clock this morning."[35]

After thirty-five years, John Hurt heard another fateful knock on the door. He later said he thought it was the FBI. Hoskins introduced himself and produced the tattered copy of "Avalon Blues." He asked, "Can you play that song?"

Hurt replied, "I could if I had a guitar."

Hoskins was happy to oblige. He went out to the car and brought back his Gibson, inlaid with stars and moons in mother-of-pearl. Hurt cradled it in his hands. It was soon obvious that there wasn't much dust on the magical, intricate riffs. He glided through the repertoire, only heard before on scratchy 78s. "Do you know how famous you are?" Hoskins asked. Hurt didn't, but he would.

Later that summer, Spottswood had John Hurt put in as a last-minute program addition to the 1963 Newport Folk Festival. Hurt had stumbled into the epicenter of American music. Folk was at its zenith with Joan Baez and Peter, Paul, and Mary. Baez introduced a skinny kid from Minnesota named Bob Dylan there. They joined Dylan on stage for "Blowing in the Wind." "We Shall Overcome" became the anthem of the Civil Rights Movement.

In the middle of all this, Dick Spottswood introduced an old Black man in a fedora to an impossibly young, predominantly white audience on a bright, perfect July day. The new act was a small man with a well-muscled neck and chest from a life of hard work. The stage was like a bigger version of the front porch at the Valley Store. Emerging blues stars John Hammond and John Lee Hooker could be seen on the stage behind. There was scarcely room to move. The crowd was packed in around him, on folding chairs and standing, nodding along with the opening riffs. John Hurt was beaming.

"It's been quite a while since I did this, and I'm real happy to be here with y'all. You know I can't help but be happy."

At seventy, he was the surprise hit of the festival. The next three years would bring college concerts, coffee shop gigs, and record deals. John Sebastian named his band The Lovin' Spoonful, after a line in Hurt's "Coffee Blues." Hurt played Carnegie Hall and appeared with Johnny Carson on *The Tonight Show*. The music world embraced him four decades after fame had flitted away.

But the traveling and touring may have taken a toll. Hurt moved to Washington, to better manage his career after Hoskins's original contact, but it was a brief stay. Too far from his roots, he moved back to Mississippi. In 1966, on a hunting trip in the woods of Avalon, John Hurt died from a stroke at seventy-three.

After more dirt roads through the hills, Floyd's truck pulled up in front of a well-patched house in a clearing. The wooden sign on the front read: MISSISSIPPI JOHN HURT MUSEUM. It's Hurt's original Avalon home, a narrow house with interconnected rooms, of that style of African American origin known as a "shotgun." Although it's said these are called shotgun houses because a bullet fired through the front door would go right out the back without hitting a wall, evidence suggests that the name may be a corruption of the word "shogon." Among the Yoruba of West Africa, "shogon" means "God's House."

Old steel wagon wheels and a rocking chair graced the porch, and termites seemed to have made some progress on the floor joists. Floyd unlocked the door for us. It was all inside: the guitars, the *Life* magazine article from the '60s, the proclamation from the governor, and the photos of a small man who made his living cutting railroad ties and playing the blues.

Floyd had to leave, and he locked up the house. He told us we could stay as long as we liked, and we watched the old pickup disappear back into the woods. "Mind if we hang out a little?" Rick asked.

Rick went back to the car and pulled his guitar case out of the trunk. He settled in on the porch of the shotgun, taking his time to tune the guitar, as though this were his biggest gig. He started in on a slow walk through his repertoire of Mississippi John Hurt songs. Rick's baritone trickled out into the deep oak forest. Maybe Avalon, Mississippi, is not so far from King Arthur's magical island.

Rick Sullivan at the Mississippi John Hurt Museum, Avalon, Mississippi.

iv. Ulysses Grant and the Opening of the Underground Railroad (Mississippi, Tennessee)

Riding north through Mississippi and Tennessee, Rick and I gradually realized that we were in the footsteps of a quiet man with piercing dark gray eyes. Ulysses Grant's Army of the Tennessee was the mighty hammer smashing the Confederacy in the west and opening a path to freedom for thousands upon thousands of the enslaved. As a result of Grant's drive into the South, freedom seekers would no longer need the Underground Railroad to reach Canada, or even the free states. They would only have to reach the Union lines. It became vastly easier to make a run for a new life.

Our route took us northward, the opposite direction from Grant's army, so we encountered the sites of Grant's great battles in the reverse order that they happened: Vicksburg, the great citadel on the Mississippi River; Shiloh, where the true toll of the Civil War would be revealed; and Fort Donelson, the first major Union victory.

We approached Grant's road on a 72-mile day across southern Mississippi on remote roads through deep forest and hard-luck towns. We arrived after dinner in Natchez, a town that epitomized what Grant's army would ultimately destroy. The motel owner opened the barbecue place next door just for us and even drove Rick to pick up a six-pack. Before the Civil War, Natchez held more millionaires per capita than anywhere in America.[36] Since 1934, the grand mansions of Natchez have been the object of elaborate house tours. Greek Revival estates dot the city. The men who owned them held hundreds, sometimes thousands, of people in bondage. The enslaved built and maintained the houses.[37]

The source of that wealth was the sale of multitudes of people, placing Natchez behind only New Orleans as a trading center. The bustling market was discretely sited at the edge of town. Our motel was just a mile from the Forks of the Road, a grassy patch between two busy highways where the slave pens once stood. A modest US Park Service kiosk there marks the spot.

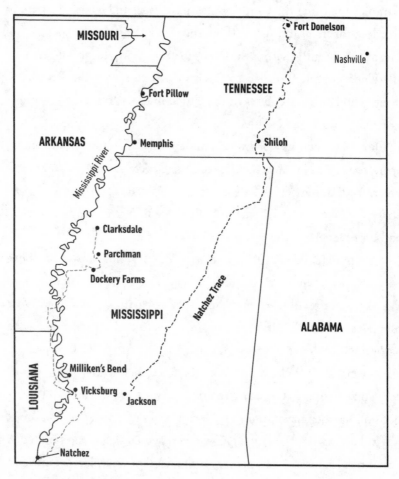

Major battles of Grant's Army of the Tennessee (Fort Donelson, Shiloh, Vicksburg) and the US Colored Troops (Milliken's Bend, Fort Pillow). Bicycle routes shown in heavy dash (2015) and light dash (2017).

SLAVES! SLAVES!! SLAVES!!!
FORKS OF THE ROAD, NATCHEZ.
THE SUBSCRIBERS have just arrived
in Natchez, and are now stopping at Mr. Elam's
house, Forks of the Foad, with a choice selection
of slaves, consisting of
MECHANICS,
    FIELD HANDS,
        COOKS,
           WASHERS AND IRONERS, and
              GENERAL HOUSE SERVANTS.
They will be constantly receiving additions to their
present supply during the season, and will be sold at as
reasonable rates as can be afforded in this market.
☞ To those purchasers desiring it, the Louisiana
guarantee will be given.
Planters and others desirous of purchasing, are re-
quested to call and see the Slaves before purchasing
elsewhere.   nov27—d:wtf   GRIFFIN & PULLUM.

Advertisement for Forks of the Road in the Natchez
Daily Courier, November 28, 1858.[38]

We rode to the nearby start of the Natchez Trace Parkway, a beautiful 444-mile road that follows an old trading route. It's a perfect
route for cycling, with low traffic and a good surface. "Trace" was the
colonial word for a Native trail through a forest, and originally this
was a trail of the Natchez people, before it became the major trade
road from Nashville to Natchez. The air was heavy and buggy, the
flora explosive. Off the Trace are cypress swamps, with "knees" from
the trees protruding above the water. Alligator habitat, so we were
told. The forest primeval. Cypress trees often reach six hundred years
in age. They have seen it all.

Off in the woods, one can find remnants of the original trail, a deep
cut between high banks, perhaps ten feet wide. The signs refer to it
variously as The Sunken Trace or The Old Trace. In places it's like a

tunnel through the forest, with saplings growing in the middle and cobwebs hanging from branches.

A section of the old Natchez Trace, the road worn deep
into the forest by thousands of chained feet.

The Trace was a major artery of commerce, with traders from the Ohio Valley floating down the Mississippi with boatloads of goods, selling their boats, then returning up the Trace by land. But the Trace carried another kind of commerce. This was one of the principal routes for slave coffles, as the Forks of the Road were "constantly receiving additions to their present supply." Located outside of Washington, in Alexandria, Virginia, the firm of Franklin & Armfield was the largest trading operation, trafficking as many as a thousand people a year, with many if not most coming down the Trace.

There were independent operators as well. In 1811, the year of the Charles Deslondes revolt, Andrew Jackson, then a Nashville lawyer and slave trader, led a coffle of enslaved people along the Trace. He was stopped by a federal agent and asked to produce ownership papers. Flying into a rage, he produced a copy of the US Constitution, which he said was a "sufficient passport to take me wherever my business leads me." After being allowed to pass, Jackson launched a letter campaign that ultimately led to the agent's removal, asking in one petition, "Are we freemen or are we slaves?"[39]

Walking along the Sunken Trace, I thought of a place on the other side of the continent. In eastern Oregon, I've seen the ruts of wagon trains on the Oregon Trail still visible in the dry sagebrush. Here in the deep forest of Mississippi, one can find still visible another piece of American history. Many wagons came down this road, but the deeply recessed scar through the forest is also the product of tens of thousands of chained feet. This is a rare place, in Morrison's words, to "think about or not think about, to summon the presences of, or recollect the absences of slaves."

The Trace can be remote, and it's not necessarily easy to find a place for lunch. Google showed us only one spot anywhere near our route. Just a mile off the Parkway, a well-patched little country store appeared out of the forest. Rick and I stretched our legs on the porch and had a leisurely lunch. The owner told us that the Old Crossroads Store had been standing for 160 years, since before the Civil War. Out in front, a plaque read: GRANT'S MARCH. It was our first crossing of the track of an iron will from a century and a half ago. Ulysses Grant would be our companion from here on, and the Vicksburg Campaign, of which this was a part, was his masterwork.

Someone sitting out on that porch in May 1863 would have heard them before seeing them: a rustle of boots, a clank of canteens, a clop of hooves. The sea of forty thousand dusty, blue-uniformed soldiers tramped by for hours. The Federals wore belt buckles that read U.S., perhaps just as easily standing for Ulysses S. or Unconditional Surrender. Whatever the abbreviation, what marched by the Crossroads Store that day, not a mile from where the coffles dragged their sorrow through the forest, was the terrible swift sword.

Grant rode by on that day, likely in a dirty uniform and a slouch hat. In the accounts of his contemporaries, what was striking about Grant was how unremarkable he appeared. People described him as taciturn, low-key, enigmatic. He was in the bottom half of his class at West Point but fought valiantly in the Mexican War. When he resigned from the army, he needed to borrow money from a fellow West Pointer, Simon Bolivar Buckner, to return home. Grant drank, though far less than later newspapers would claim. He had failed as a farmer and a real estate agent and was working as a clerk at his father's business at the time of Fort Sumter's fall in April 1861. Seven years after leaving the army, he answered Lincoln's call for volunteers and soon brought a brigade of new recruits into fighting shape. Some would notice those intense gray eyes.

Grant held curious views for the man who would become the nation's principal instrument of liberation. He married an enslaver and was one himself in the years before the war. As the war approached, Grant speculated in a letter to his father that after the abolitionist Republicans had taken over, the market for slaves would bottom out and "the n[____] will never disturb this country again."[40] Yet his views would change.

In that marker at the Crossroads Store was a demonstration of a dominant trait of his character: an almost superhuman perseverance. Everyone knew that the capture of Vicksburg was the key to victory in the west, none more so than Abraham Lincoln, who had gazed up at the city's towering bluffs as he twice floated past on flatboats as a young man. Grant's first efforts to take the city were met with failure upon failure. A direct assault was thrown back, as well as an attempt to send gunboats through the bayous north of town. His men twice tried to dig a canal to reroute the great Mississippi River around the citadel. His final audacious plan involved sailing his gunboat fleet under the guns of the citadel, landing his army across the river south of the city, and marching in a giant fishhook to trap the Confederate Army in a siege. The march by the Crossroads Store was part of that fishhook. The plan entailed the army leaving its supply lines and losing contact with Washington. Grant likely welcomed the latter.

Meanwhile a remarkable change was happening in the conduct of the war. On a raid into the Delta, one of Grant's commanders, Frederick Steele, remarked on the waves of the formerly enslaved following his force. The Underground Railroad now ended with the Union Army. Steele tried to convince them to stay where they were, writing to Grant, "What shall be done with these poor creatures?" Grant's reply stunned him. He told Steele to "encourage all negroes, particularly middle-aged males, to come within our lines."[41] He had started to form Black regiments, the US Colored Troops, and they would begin to change the course of the war.

Rick and I turned off the Natchez Trace and headed to Vicksburg for a rest day. We might have thought twice about that had we known of Vicksburg's other nickname: along with "Gibraltar of the Confederacy" (as in a great fortress), it's also called "The Hill City." We spent the day crawling up and down those hills on our bikes, through the forts and siege works still in place as part of the National Battlefield Park. At the end of the great campaign, Grant's army held the city and its defenses in a death grip. On July 4, 1863, the day after the battle of Gettysburg, the Gibraltar of the Confederacy surrendered.

The year before, Grant had pressed his invasion from the north, with a great smoky armada of gunboats and transports chugging south on the Tennessee River. His Army of the Tennessee landed just below Savannah, not far from the Mississippi border. There the army paused to await a second force, under Don Carlos Buell, marching from the east. The question was whether the Confederates would wait.

At the most exposed position in the Union encampment were troops under William Tecumseh Sherman. A captain in the Ohio cavalry on a scouting expedition reported the presence of a large Confederate force two miles distant. Sherman replied, "Oh tut-tut. You militia officers get scared too easy." He even chided the officer for running the risk of drawing the army into a fight before it was ready. The battle would come whether the army was ready or not. Sherman's headquarters was at a little church known as Shiloh, which in Hebrew means "place of peace."[42]

Rick and I approached Shiloh from the south, banging up our share of hills. The Natchez Trace was easy for bicycles if not for the enslaved. But after leaving the friendly confines of the Parkway, we were faced with more typical Mississippi roads: two-lane roads with dirt shoulders and drivers not inclined to give cyclists any quarter. Rick remembers hearing a rumbling behind him, then turning to see the black lettering on the yellow background of a school bus inches from his face.

Our accommodations were getting sparse by the time we reached northern Mississippi. The motel in Iuka didn't look impressive from the outside, apparently a single room occupancy place. The small parking lot was littered with rebar and jagged chunks of concrete. I started talking with the owner, and Rick was getting increasingly anxious about staying there. He had what he thought was a brilliant idea and asked the owner if we could see the room before making a decision. The owner unlocked the door. The room had vinyl fake wood paneling, stained covers, a gritty floor, and a good-sized hole in the bathroom wall. Rick was thinking we'd dodged a bullet.

"This will be fine," I said. Rick was gobsmacked.

"I'm not criticizing your standards," he later told me, "I just haven't been able to detect any."

Crossing into Tennessee in a little creek bottom, Rick was in the lead when a pack of dogs rushed out of one of the roadside houses. I got my pepper spray out quickly, but they were surrounding us, snarling and snapping, before I could get off the first shot. One planted itself firmly in Rick's path. Rick screamed at him, hoping he would move. He did. Yelling and pepper spray got us out quickly enough, but we were both shaken.

We proceeded to prove that it is possible to get lost even with GPS, especially when there's no signal. We were floundering through a scrub pine forest in dry, dusty Tennessee clay on a potholed road. Each wrong turn brought another climb in the thick heat. At the top of a hill, we asked directions of a man in a pickup. He wore a US Park Service uniform, a good omen. Backtracking down the hill and around a few curves, the rutted pavement suddenly turned smooth. We were at once exhausted and awed. By the side of the road was a monument with a small obelisk and stacked cannonballs. And a sign: ENTERING SHILOH NATIONAL MILITARY PARK. We were just emerging from a forest.

At the edge of that same forest on a Sunday morning in April 1862, Union troops were just sitting down to breakfast when the commotion happened. First deer, then rabbits and quail came running and flying through the campsite. Someone must have been thinking *This can't be good*, right before they heard the first rebel yell. Sherman had ignored all the warnings.

The Confederate attack smashed the Union encampment, driving the soldiers back toward the Tennessee River for most of the day. One

Union division made a stand at a place that became known as the Hornets' Nest. They were pummeled, surrounded, and captured, but in slowing the Confederate advance they would buy the Union Army just enough time to survive. By the end of the day, Grant held a thin sliver of ground near the river at Pittsburgh Landing while waiting for Buell's army. The author Ambrose Bierce was then an officer in Buell's force, crossing the river to the landing late that afternoon. The air was full of smoke, and flashes from the far shore lay ahead of Bierce's boat:

> A thousand lights kindled and expired every second. . . .
> Occasionally could be seen moving black figures, distinct,
> but no larger than a thumb; they seemed to be like the
> figures of demons in old allegorical prints of hell.[43]

Grant and Sherman spent the night in the headquarters camp in that desperate place. They had some history between them and were destined to make more. Grant's drinking had been the subject of rumors before the war, and Sherman was alleged to have had a nervous breakdown. After the war, Sherman would say of Grant, "He stood by me when I was crazy, and I stood by him when he was drunk, and now we stand by each other."

The words "last ditch" have a particular meaning at Shiloh. After surprising the Union Army in their dawn attack, the Confederates had a very good chance to drive it into the Tennessee River. But the hard fighting of the Federals that day prevented the retreat from becoming a rout. The Confederate attack expended itself one ravine short of the river. Thousands of frightened Union troops gathered around the riverbank landing. Sherman walked into Grant's tent that night.

"Well, Grant," Sherman said to his friend, "we've had the devil's own day, haven't we?"

"Yes," replied Grant. "Lick 'em tomorrow, though."

Maybe the war's turning point was that very moment. Many Union generals folded in just such a crucible. There was a horrendous tempest that night, a scene out of Dante. Wounded and dying men lay on the battlefield, caught in the driving rain. Grant, cool and focused, was planning the counterattack the next day, as Buell's forces piled into the landing. When dawn broke, the reinforced Union Army drove the Confederates back to roughly their original lines, not far from the forest at the entrance to Shiloh.

Shiloh was, in essence, a frighteningly bloody draw. At the end of the second day, the Confederates withdrew, and the Federals remained on the field. The Union invasion had not been stopped. But the toll that Shiloh delivered was unprecedented. That single battle produced 23,000 casualties, more men than had fallen in the Revolutionary War, the War of 1812, and the Mexican War combined. It would be just a prelude of things to come.

Outside of the Shiloh Visitor Center, a cannon marks the line of the Union's final stand on that first day of battle. Rick and I were just finishing our visit there in the late afternoon, not far from the site of Grant's headquarters tent. We saw a very different attack approaching from the south. A rumbling came from over the horizon, and the sky darkened. A check on the Doppler radar showed a bright red line of storms approaching.

"Rick, we gotta go. We gotta go."

Adrenaline again fueled a fast ride toward Savannah, Tennessee. The squall line seemed to be gaining. Then, a crackling up ahead. Storms were suddenly all around us. Rick smelled ozone, the metallic smell produced by electricity in the air. I watched the near horizon disappear as the downdraft brought the first raindrops. Time for shelter, right now. We ducked under a highway bridge as the sky exploded. The rain came in sheets, horizontally. We took extra cover behind a bridge abutment. Over our heads, a waterfall was coming down from the bridge's storm drains. As the rain slowed, we ventured out from our hiding place. The Tennessee River still lay between our motel in Savannah and us. We still needed to make Bierce's crossing, in the opposite direction.

We came out from under the overpass too soon. As we approached the Tennessee River Bridge, the rain front was moving down the river toward us. It enfolded us as we pushed up to the summit of the bridge. A sheet of water surged down the bridge deck. We pedaled up the incline like salmon swimming upstream. I yelled at Rick up ahead, "You okay?" He nodded, but he later shared what he was thinking: *No, I'm not doing too well. You want to stop and talk about it?* The motel room that night was covered with wet clothes. Exhausted, we just made last call for the kitchen at the local diner.

Dried out and marginally rested, we rode north out of Shiloh along the Cumberland River, running into one hill after another. Once upon a time, when I worked on the Louisiana oil rigs, I was talking about the Rockies when one of the local roustabouts interrupted: "Them mountains up by Shreveport are so high they'll make your nose bleed." Tennessee hills weren't quite that big but were formidable nevertheless. It would be the most climbing of any day of the 1,500-mile ride, with no food or drink anywhere along that segment of the route. Granola bars and trail mix were the menu of the day, washed down with warm tap water from the bottles.

Rick had to turn off to Nashville for his flight home, taking the motel concerts and stories of the blues with him. On the long days on the bikes, we'd made mistakes—the wrong turns, the roadside glass—but we'd tended to correct each other. The company and conversation had been lively and welcome at the end of each day. Now I was on my own. When I stumbled into Dover, the town adjacent to Fort Donelson National Battlefield Park, I was exhausted. The roadside Hillbilly Barbecue Shack was haute cuisine.

At the start of the Civil War, his commanders had seen something in Ulysses Grant. In early 1862, he was given command of an invasion force to subdue the rebellious states west of the Appalachians. The Federals had a large force of ironclad gunboats, and the Mississippi River might have been the first choice for an invasion route. But the Confederates had built great fortresses on that river, including the greatest of them all at Vicksburg. So Grant looked east, to the rivers that ran south into Kentucky and Tennessee. The hastily built Fort Henry guarded the Tennessee River, while Fort Donelson overlooked the Cumberland. Fort Henry fell rather easily to the massed fire of Union gunboats as Grant's army marched overland. Fort Donelson would be another story. Grant's army closed in by land while the smoke-belching gunboats came down the Cumberland in mid-February. What they delivered became known as "Iron Valentines."

Atop a hill lay Fort Donelson. I walked around the battlefield as late afternoon light cast long shadows over little knolls and ridges, the still-preserved Confederate trenches surrounding the fort. Looking out above the river were gun emplacements, where in 1862 the rebels waited for what was coming up the river. They could see the smoke rising from around the next bend before their first view of the iron monsters.

But the Yankee gunboats would not have as easy a time as at Fort Henry. Three of the four vessels were disabled by the ferocious artillery coming down on them from the bluff. Grant surveyed the scene as they retreated. The battle would be up to his army, which then moved up to surround the fort. The siege and fighting lasted but two days. Given the unpleasant duty of surrender was Confederate general Simon Bolivar Buckner, Grant's West Point friend and lender. Buckner sent a message asking for "appointment of commissioners to agree upon terms of capitulation."

Chivalry was not Ulysses S. Grant's long suit. The night was growing icy as he entered the headquarters tent. He was stiff from the cold and exhausted from watching the slaughter. He asked for a drink; a flask appeared. He chuckled a bit in contemplating a response to Buckner. He picked up a pen. "No terms except an immediate and unconditional surrender can be accepted. I propose to move immediately upon your works."

Buckner was furious, but he complied. It was the first significant Union victory of the war after a string of humiliating losses. The Northern press would anoint their new hero "Unconditional Surrender Grant." But a key figure escaped from the trap at Fort Donelson, and that would come back to haunt Grant. That night Nathan Bedford Forrest and his cavalry slipped unseen through the Union lines.

The park ranger at the information desk said, a little defensively, "We get a lot of questions about Forrest." He was probably the best Confederate general in the west, fighting with energy and brute courage. He would harass and outmaneuver Union forces for the next three years. He was also a former slave trader. Two years after Fort Donelson, he and his cavalry came upon an obscure Union emplacement on the Mississippi called Fort Pillow, whose garrison was roughly half African American. We were due to travel to Fort Pillow in a few days to reckon with what happened.

Forrest would have been particularly distressed by what had become of Fort Donelson. By virtue of Grant's victory there, the Underground Railroad was now vastly shorter and would shorten still further with each Union advance. Instead of having to travel by night all the way to and across the Ohio River, the formerly enslaved only had to reach the Union lines. Freedom was now 120 miles—and about two weeks—closer. Escaping families of the formerly enslaved, fleeing in droves, flocked to Fort Donelson seeking protection and a new life.

But in this early part of the Civil War, before the Emancipation Proclamation, these refugees presented the Union Army with a quandary. By the law of the land at the time, these people were someone's property. The Union forces came up with an ingenious solution. Since enslaved people were presumably helping in the Confederate war effort, they could be declared "contraband of war" and recruited to help the Union cause. "Contraband camps," while grating to the modern ear, nevertheless became ubiquitous in lands newly seized from the Confederacy. By March 1863 some three hundred refugees lived at the freedmen's camp near Fort Donelson that came to be known as "Free State." Many of the men enlisted in the Union Army, as Union States Colored Troops, after Fort Donelson became an army recruiting station for African Americans in November 1863. Some may have been at Fort Pillow.

Sometime after the ride, I came across Grant's path once more, in downtown Washington. There is a fine old bar, a place of dark, polished wood and famous faces on the wall, known as the Round Robin, just off the lobby of the Willard Hotel. Right around the corner from the White House, it was the haunt of Lincoln and Grant, of Walt Whitman and Mark Twain. It was a slow day as the bartender spun me a story. He pointed to the wall.

Right over there used to be the women's entrance to the bar. On Good Friday 1865, General Grant is having a drink in those heady days right after Appomattox. Julia Grant comes right through that door and announces that she doesn't want to go to the play that night. Seems she and Mary Todd Lincoln don't get along very well. The General has to make some sort of sheepish excuse to the White House. He and Mrs. Grant are headed down Pennsylvania Avenue in their carriage when a man with a handlebar mustache comes galloping up, leans over and stares right at them. The man then turns and rides away. That's how John Wilkes Booth learns for sure that Grant would not be in the president's box at Ford's Theatre that night.

It wouldn't be Grant's last visit to the Willard. During his presidency, those seeking Grant's ear would come to the lobby of the Willard, where he would often have his whiskey. The visitors would be known as lobbyists. The caricature of his presidency was one stained by corruption and cronyism. There was never any intimation that he personally profited from the various payoffs. But one quotation is revealing: "I have made it the rule of my life to trust a man long after other people gave him up."

After leaving the presidency, Grant put his trust in one Ferdinand Ward, then known as the "Young Napoleon of Finance." The firm of Grant and Ward opened an office at 2 Wall Street, and Julia and Ulysses enjoyed the company of some of the nation's richest financiers. On a Tuesday in 1884, Grant's son brought him the news: "The bank has failed. Ward has fled. We cannot find our securities." The family was bankrupt immediately. The firm's cashier caught a glimpse of Grant that afternoon as he sat with his hands gripping the arms of a chair, his face expressionless.[44]

His cancer diagnosis would come two months later. Writing his memoirs had always been his intention, but the urgency was now pronounced. Mark Twain, about to release *Huckleberry Finn*, took on the publication of the volume. Grant secluded himself in a cottage in the Adirondacks and began to write in earnest. At the end of each day, he took brandy and morphine to dull the pain. He wrote the two-volume *Complete Personal Memoirs of Ulysses S. Grant* in nine months, finishing three days before his death.[45] It would be one of the bestsellers of the nineteenth century, providing support for his family after his passing.

His former opponents at Fort Donelson followed divergent paths. Simon Buckner was not one to hold grudges after the "unconditional surrender" there. He would become governor of Kentucky and converse with Grant via notes in Grant's final days at the Adirondack cottage. He would be one of Grant's pallbearers at the 1885 funeral. Nathan Bedford Forrest would be the first Grand Wizard of the Ku Klux Klan.

Today, with the fading of the Lost Cause narrative of the Civil War, Grant's stock as president has risen markedly. In my high school history class in Virginia, the Civil War was the "War Between the States," Grant's presidency was "scandal-ridden," and Reconstruction was the time of carpetbaggers, the *Gone with the Wind* narrative. Today, Reconstruction, over which Grant presided, is increasingly seen as the first civil rights movement, only to be swept away later by violence and the advent of the Jim Crow laws. During his presidency, Grant took the protection of the four million formerly enslaved new citizens quite seriously. He repeatedly sent federal troops south to protect them. He was the major force behind the Ku Klux Klan Act, which brought more than a thousand convictions and at least temporarily suppressed the Klan. Historian Eric Foner refers to Reconstruction as "the Second Founding."

How did Grant, who wrote about "the n＿ problem" before the war, come to be first the leader of the instrument of liberation and later the defender of that liberation? What changed his mind? After Fort Donelson, he looked out on the waves of freed people surging to the Union lines in the now-shortened Underground Railroad. Before and after Vicksburg, he sought ways to use what his subordinate called "wretched souls" in service of the Union cause. Grant wasn't simply following Lincoln's policy; he was carrying it out enthusiastically. In a letter back to Washington, Grant wrote, "At least three of my Army Corps Commanders take hold of the new policy of arming the negroes and using them against the rebels with a will."[46] But a question remained: would the new recruits of the US Colored Troops fight? For Grant in 1863, one answer came from across the Mississippi River, on an obscure battlefield that no longer exists: Milliken's Bend.

v. Trial of the African Brigade (Louisiana)

Two years after our ride through Tennessee, Rick and I waited on a bright, hot spring morning on the river at Vicksburg. Crossing the Mississippi was a formidable barrier for cyclists, as it had been for

Ulysses Grant. Two bridges span the river at Vicksburg. The I-20 bridge carries four lanes of high-speed traffic, with no room for bikes. Next to it is the Vicksburg Bridge, a beautiful old cantilever structure that carries trains but doesn't allow pedestrians or bikes. After a bit of negotiation over the phone, Barry, Dustin, Larry, and Warren—the work crew from the Vicksburg Bridge Commission—let us throw our bikes in the back of their truck to take us across the great river, from its namesake state into Louisiana.

Below us, a tug pushing a string of barges labored against the current. Eddies swirled in the stream below the city. The country is flat for miles around, but we could see where guns perched on Vicksburg's bluffs once controlled the river. President Lincoln recognized its importance from his journeys in younger days: "Vicksburg is the key. The war can never be brought to a close until that key is in our pocket."

Rick and I had crossed the Mississippi looking for another battlefield, one far less well known than the fortress on the river. Before our journey across the river, at the Visitor Center at Vicksburg National Military Park, I noticed a panel display about Milliken's Bend, a mere skirmish compared to the great siege that was Vicksburg. Scarcely 1,500 men were involved on each side, but with a difference: Milliken's Bend was one of the very first battles in which Black troops fought. The site of the battle didn't appear to be far off our route, so I asked the ranger for directions. She told us that it wasn't there. In one of the great floods of the intervening 154 years, the river had swallowed up the site of Milliken's Bend. (See Major Battles of Grant's Army of the Tennessee map, page 142.)

Once over the bridge, the hills of Vicksburg transitioned to the flats of Louisiana. Rick and I had gotten used to each other's traveling styles, and we were like Huck and Jim on the river, freed from the constraints of everyday lives, waiting for the next adventure. We flew through fifty miles before stopping at one of my certified low-budget motels in Lake Providence. As I stood outside the motel room, near sunset, talking with Concetta on the phone, the curtain was rising on a big lightning show to the west. I cut the call short as the wind began to spin sand and grit up from the parking lot. As I hurried back inside, the rain started coming in sheets against the window. The lights flickered and failed; the power would stay out all night. The phones were our only lights, and we kept them plugged into the laptop, which became our lifeboat in keeping them charged. Something big was banging against the wall outside.

Rick remembers, "A South Asian couple ran the place. Right after that first wave of storms, it's all dark and the power's out, there's a knock on the door. It's the wife, and she's come to check up on us. Can you imagine that happening in a motel?"

We opened the door to the morning light, and debris was strewn everywhere around the still-dark motel. Across flooded fields, telephone poles were at odd angles, some snapped. A tornado or something very much like it had passed through that night. We pedaled gently down the road, dodging tree branches and power lines. Remarkably, we found a cafe in town that still had power. On the outskirts of town was the Louisiana State Cotton Museum, dedicated to the town's cash crop, then and now.

In the spring of 1863, this town of Lake Providence was fertile ground for the recruitment of Black soldiers. In the Emancipation Proclamation of that New Year's Day, President Lincoln declared that "such [freedmen] of suitable condition will be received into the armed service of the United States to garrison forts, positions, stations, and other places." From the cotton fields of Lake Providence came the formerly enslaved, abandoned by those who had held them in bondage in the face of advancing Union troops. The newly freed formed the 9th and 11th Louisiana Infantries (African Descent)— the African Brigade.[47] They would later be known as soldiers of the US Colored Troops. Few expected more than garrison duty for the African Brigade. They would find themselves on the levee at Milliken's Bend.

Black soldiers in blue coats with gold buttons: it was the embodiment of a dream for the abolitionists of the time. On one of his many recruiting drives, Fredrick Douglass said:

> Once let the black man get upon his person the brass letters,
> U.S., let him get an eagle on his button, and a musket on
> his shoulder and bullets in his pockets, and there can be
> no power on earth which can deny that he has earned the
> right to citizenship in the United States.[48]

But the specter of the newly freed in uniform with guns was the essence of an old nightmare of the antebellum South. In 1860, Stephen Hale, the secessionist commissioner from Alabama, laid out the consequences in starkest terms: "The dark pall of barbarism" would cast its shadow all across the South, bringing with it "the scenes of West India [Haiti] emancipation, with its attendant horrors and crimes." Memories of the Haitian slave revolt, together with those of Charles Deslondes and Nat Turner, cast a long shadow. In response to the Emancipation Proclamation, the Confederate Congress passed a resolution bringing the death penalty to Union officers making efforts to bring on "servile war," i.e., recruiting freedmen into the army. Captured Black soldiers would be treated as slaves in rebellion, with execution or re-enslavement as the likely outcome.[49]

After emancipation, what in fact transpired was far different from the nightmare. The formerly enslaved who were within a few days' journey of Union lines simply walked away. Stepping out onto the roads, they had little need for an Underground Railroad. They were interested in freedom, not revenge. Many would join the Union Army, seen as the instrument of their liberation. With the dire consequences if captured, their motivation to fight was strong indeed.

But in the emancipation year of 1863, much of the Union leadership questioned if the US Colored Troops would have either the capacity or the will to fight. The whole notion of Black men in the Union Army was hard to fathom at the time. As Ta-Nehisi Coates said, "The expectations were so low. The idea that Black people would fight as soldiers . . . this was like a man going to the moon."[50]

In the spring of 1863, Grant began his long, roundabout campaign to capture Vicksburg by landing his army in Louisiana, at Milliken's Bend. Left to guard his supply base there as his army marched south was the Northeast Louisiana District of the US African Brigade. This force of roughly 1,100 newly freed men had left the cotton fields of Lake Providence, and had carried weapons for only days or weeks. By June 7, Grant's army had laid siege to Vicksburg for three weeks. The Confederates grew desperate to unleash the city from his grip. They came to attack the supply base.

The force of Texans advancing on Milliken's Bend had their own notions of "servile insurrection." Seven years before, in Colorado County, southeast of Austin, rumors of an uprising had been rampant. Like most plots described in the press, it was said that all white men were to be killed, with women spared to become wives of the slaves in rebellion. Vigilantism became rampant. Two of the enslaved died from beatings, while three were hanged. From this county came a company of the Texas infantry that would fight on the levee at Milliken's Bend.[51]

At dawn on June 7, 1863, the men of the African Brigade stood behind felled trees and cotton bales, alerted by the crackling of gunfire as the pickets on the outskirts of the line were driven in. Now they could make out shapes, wraiths advancing in the half-light. The feared rebels, their enslavers, were coming for them. Waiting on the levee, watching the Confederates press forward, their backs were to the wall or, in this case, the river. This was the ragged edge of both desperation and fury. Those emotions cannot be uncommon for soldiers in trenches. But for the African Brigade, defeat would mean death or slavery or worse.

As the line of Texans moved through the field, the African Brigade opened fire, but most of their shots went into the air, according to their officers. Before many of the novice soldiers could reload, the Confederates were among them. The Black soldiers' musket fire was ineffective, but it was a different story as the two lines crashed together. This fight for survival required no training. It was a brawl with bayonets and swinging muskets. As their position was overrun, the battle became a fierce hand-to-hand struggle.[52]

We know a good bit about the white officers of the African Brigade, but little about the Black soldiers. One we do know about was "Big Jack" Jackson. At six-foot-six, he never wore shoes because of the size of his feet. The story is that he fled Mississippi after a fight with his overseer, killing him with one blow. After coming to the Union Army to drive mules, he joined the new brigade at the first chance. His officer saw him last on the levee, lunging into the melee, swinging his rifle butt despite his mortal wounds.[53] The Black Achilles was lost in the battle.

The Union forces were driven back to a second levee at the river, then to the riverbank. But they had slowed the Confederate wave just enough. Two Union gunboats, *Choctaw* and *Lexington*, arrived on the scene with the battle laid out in front of them. They trained their heavy guns on the Confederate lines. Meanwhile, two companies of the African Brigade managed to hold their position for the entire morning. By midmorning, the Texans had retired from the field, never reaching the supply base.[54]

Observers walking the battlefield later could see the results of its savagery. "After it was over, many men were found dead with bayonet stabs, and other with their skulls broken open by the butts of muskets," one man described.[55] The African Brigade suffered a loss of 43 percent killed, wounded, or missing, a heavy loss even by Civil War standards.

In one of their first engagements, Black soldiers demonstrated that they would fight. Prior to Milliken's Bend, racial stereotypes dominated opinions of the US Colored Troops: they were seen variously as lazy and feebleminded or tribally crazed and bloodthirsty. After the battle, Union general Elias Dennis said, "It is impossible for men to show greater gallantry than the Negro troops in this fight." More importantly, their commanding general took notice. Grant wrote:

> This was the first important engagement of the war in which colored troops were under fire. These men were very raw, having all been enlisted since the beginning of the siege, but they behaved well. They have been most gallant and I doubt not but with good officers they will make good troops.[56]

By the end of the Civil War, more than 209,000 Black soldiers and sailors would serve the Union cause, turning the tide in a North weary of war and casualty lists. They were not drafted. They were not fighting for a country. They were not citizens. More than once they were relegated to hopeless, fatal assaults. They fought for a cause, pure and simple, to strike back at a system that had controlled them since before they first opened their eyes. The accounts of the Milliken's Bend battlefield are a testament to their fury.

Rick and I tried to find Milliken's Bend, or to get as close as we could on our bikes. On a long, hot day, we stopped for barbecue at a shop with black-painted cinder block walls in the nearby town of

Tallulah. We asked about the battle site. No one seemed to have heard of it. After lunch, we located the road passing closest to what remained of the site but received a verdict from a local farmer in a pickup truck: "Rough, rough, rough. Bits of pavement, potholes, gravel. Y'all will end up walking it." But not far down the main road sat a faded display panel: "Freedmen Fight at Milliken's Bend," telling the story of the African Brigade.

Roadside panel near Delta, Louisiana.

Milliken's Bend is little known today, and it's not surprising that it came to be forgotten like so many other markers of Black history. Louisiana after the Civil War became a deadly place for the formerly enslaved. Racial violence was so omnipresent in 1868, just three years after the end of the Civil War, that the Freedman's Bureau assistant commissioner for the state of Louisiana filled an entire ledger book in the category "Outrages and Murders" in a mere six months.[57] Two hours west of Tallulah is Colfax, where in 1873 a white mob killed between sixty-two and eighty-three Black men trying to defend the local integrated government.[58] The narrative of Black heroes would not find fertile ground there.

This first battle—and victory—of the African Brigade seems to have been washed from the recollections of the locals and from history at large, much like the river washed the battlefield away. But perhaps the river holds its own memories. In 1995, Toni Morrison wrote an essay called "The Site of Memory," observing:

> You know, they straightened out the Mississippi River in places to make room for houses and livable acreage. Occasionally the river floods these places. "Floods" is the word they use, but in fact it is not flooding; it is remembering. Remembering where it used to be.[59]

vi. The Sunflower Field (Tennessee)

We loaded the bicycles in the back of the rental car. Rick and I had ridden over 500 miles from New Orleans, up the river, past Milliken's Bend, to the Delta Blues town of Clarksdale. We were ready to drive back east and finish the long journey. Fifty-mile cycling days in the heat had worn on both of us. But on the way home, we decided to stop by an old Civil War site, the stuff of headlines a century and a half ago, now all but forgotten. Buried in the backwoods north of Memphis is a Tennessee state park so remote that even the Mississippi River doesn't visit anymore. We left our car and went in search of the fort. We padded down a forest path for about a mile then came upon a hilltop fortification, cannons pointed through ports in a grassy wall.

After looking at the plaques and narratives at the Fort Pillow Visitors' Center, we tried to use their map to pace out how the battle had unfolded. Something was missing. We went down the bluff to the water's edge, to the oxbow lake where the Mississippi once flowed. As at Milliken's Bend, the river had changed its path over the intervening century and a half. A couple of peaceful summer cabins were set back from the water. Stretching out from a boat ramp was a field of thinleaf sunflowers, fading off into the woods. The sunflowers waved in a gentle breeze. A glance down at the map, another look up, a shudder. This was a place of unspeakable horror.

Ten months after Milliken's Bend, freedmen were streaming into the Union lines and into units of the US Colored Troops. From the perspective of the Confederacy, perhaps they needed to be taught a lesson. Who better to deliver such a lesson than a former slave trader and one of its most competent generals?

A long, desperate road led Nathan Bedford Forrest to Fort Pillow in April 1864. Forrest was the brilliant and mercurial Confederate cavalry commander of the west, who became known as "The Wizard of the Saddle." He had risen from childhood in a log cabin to become one of the richest men in Tennessee, making his fortune before the war in the Memphis slave trade. He joined the Confederate Army as a private and rose to the rank of lieutenant general. A biographer described him as two different men: "a soft-spoken gentleman of marked placidity and an overbearing bully of homicidal wrath."[60] His photographs reveal a dark visage, and at six-foot-two he was a giant for his time. His reputation generated fear from both the opposing Union forces and his own men—not necessarily a bad trait for a general. His weapon of choice was the lightning cavalry raid, his forces seemingly appearing out of nowhere. Lacking formal military training, he still had an instinct for a basic military doctrine: get there "first with the most men."

Earlier in the war, Ulysses Grant's forces had trapped Forrest, along with a substantial Confederate force, at Fort Donelson, further east in Tennessee (chapter 3.iv). After learning of the impending surrender, Forrest had led his cavalry out through the Union lines in the small hours of the morning. Grant came to regret that escape.

We continued to push north ourselves. We were drawn by the big city: Memphis. Rick knows history well, and throughout our journey, he had kept his eye on one date: April 4th. On that afternoon we walked into Memphis's National Civil Rights Museum, built onto the Lorraine Motel, site of Martin Luther King Jr.'s assassination. This was the forty-ninth anniversary.

The Lorraine is a place stopped in time, a 1960s-era motel straight out of *The Negro Travelers' Green Book*. The streaming late afternoon sun cast long shadows. A choir sang sweet gospel music. Orators spoke King's soaring words from the black-creped motel balcony, followed by a moment of silence at 6:04 P.M. It was a moment both dark and light.

The crowd drifted off into the evening. Over dinner, Rick confessed: "I'm drained." Our conversation wandered back through the emotional day, and we decided that we had one more stop yet to make, on the following day, to a place fully dark. Somehow Fort Pillow seemed like the logical last stop on our way home.

In the spring of 1864, during the waning days of the Civil War, Nathan Bedford Forrest was one of the last remaining hopes for the South. Fort Pillow was one of many battles for Forrest's cavalry, but unlike all the others, this place was garrisoned largely by the newly established US Colored Troops. As at Milliken's Bend, many had recently been enslaved. Their shortened Underground Railroad led them here.

In 1864, the year after Vicksburg and Milliken's Bend, several mortal blows were aimed at the Confederacy. One was from William Tecumseh Sherman's army, preparing to drive from Tennessee through Georgia. Forrest needed to divert strength and attention from Sherman's march to the sea, so he launched an attack into Union-held Kentucky. After striking Paducah, Kentucky, Forrest turned his attention south to Tennessee, to the lightly held Fort Pillow on the Mississippi. He left history no clues to his motives, but he surely knew that Fort Pillow was held predominantly by Black troops. The thousands of newly freed, volunteering for the "servile war" as Union soldiers, posed an increasingly severe threat. Perhaps he thought that a strike against Black troops would give their recruiters pause. Or perhaps he merely saw the fort as an easy target.

On the morning of April 12th, Forrest's troops approached the fort. They outnumbered the fort's defenders by almost three to one. Confederate sharpshooters acquired a hilltop position looking into the fort. The Union commander, Lionel Booth, was one of the first casualties of the fight. The fort was quickly surrounded. Under a flag of truce, Forrest demanded the fort's surrender, writing, "I have received a new supply of ammunition and can take your works by assault, and if compelled to do so you must take the consequences."

William Bradford, the second-in-command after Booth's death, might have thought he could hold out. After asking for time, he declined to surrender. The final assault was rapid and overwhelming, as Forrest's troops poured over the grassy embankment of the fort. The Union troops retreated down the bluff toward the river under heavy fire from all sides. A Confederate sergeant wrote in a letter:

> The slaughter was awful. Words cannot describe the
> scene. The poor deluded negroes would run up to our

men, fall upon their knees and with uplifted hands scream for mercy but they were ordered to their feet and shot down. The whitte men [*sic*] fared but little better. Their fort turned out to be a great slaughter pen.[61]

But the white men did in fact fare better. A detailed study of casualty figures at Fort Pillow shows that a third of white Union soldiers were killed, while almost two-thirds (63 percent) of the Black soldiers did not survive the battle.[62] Similar reports from a Confederate newspaper correspondent and Union survivors back the claim of a massacre. General James Chalmers, Forrest's second-in-command, issued a congratulatory order when the force returned to Mississippi, stating that his men had "taught the mongrel garrison of blacks and renegades a lesson long to be remembered."[63] Only later did denials begin.

Did Forrest give the order of "No quarter"—no surrender—during the battle, as was passed along from some of the Confederate troops? There's no real evidence that he did. But when Charles Fitch, the captured Union surgeon, was brought before Forrest and denied being the Black regiment's doctor, Forrest replied, "I still have a great mind to have you killed for being down there."[64]

Many of the most heinous acts are accomplished with a wink and a nod. Forrest did not have to *say* anything. He merely had to do nothing. He appeared on the battlefield late in the day to halt firing, but by then the slaughter was nearly complete.

Rick and I wandered through the visitors' center at the park. The displays and the film highlight conflict and controversy as a legacy of the battle, citing "unusual battle conditions," including "battle fury," "force of the assault," and "drowning deaths." But the striking proportion of Black soldiers who died is undisputed. And while war crimes are a modern construct, white flags and raised hands are not. The ranger, with a shrug, said: "Who knows what happened?"

We found the ranger's and the film's explanations unsatisfying. On the question of Forrest's role, Rick shook his head: "He knew exactly what he was doing at Fort Pillow. He was the military equivalent of the natural athlete, who sees exactly what's going on during moments of high chaos and knows where to go and what to do. He knew what was going to happen down on the riverbank, and he held back." We paused to look out over the sunflowers.

In 1864, the North used the propaganda value of Fort Pillow to maximum effect. A congressional investigation brought forth a report full of lurid details picked up by the Northern newspapers. Many were unsubstantiated, but the Fort Pillow story was a potent recruiting tool. The lesson "long to be remembered" was recalled far differently than General Chalmers might have wished. In battle after battle, the call of "Remember Fort Pillow" was heard among advancing Black soldiers in the last years of the Civil War. The over 200,000 US Colored Troops may well have turned the tide for a war-weary North.

After the war, Nathan Bedford Forrest was pardoned by his fellow Tennessean, President Andrew Johnson. He would go on to become the first Grand Wizard of the Ku Klux Klan in 1866. Though officially disbanded in 1869 and disavowed by Forrest, the Klan was merely a first wave of night riders and terrorist organizations providing the muscle to enforce the emerging Jim Crow regime. The Klan itself was resurrected in 1915 after the first feature-length motion picture, *Birth of a Nation*, was screened to rave reviews at Woodrow Wilson's White House. The new mass media was remarkably effective. We forget how influential the Klan was then, extending far outside of the South. Thousands of white-robed Klansmen would parade in Washington, in 1925 and 1926.

Forrest, as an old man, surely had some second thoughts on what he had unleashed. After officially signing an order disbanding the Klan in 1869, he wrote a letter to the governor five years later offering to "exterminate" those responsible for "the cowardly murder of Negroes."[65] He even advocated for the admission of African Americans to law school, a radical position for the 1870s. He told a former aide who had not seen him in years, "I am not the same man you knew."[66] Perhaps at the end of his life he realized the evil he had unleashed. Did he seek vindication or atonement, and was he haunted by his actions? Regardless, it was too late. After the Civil War, the gray ghosts turned into night riders. And on that April day in 1864, Forrest was in command of the attacking force at Fort Pillow, and the commander is responsible for the actions of his troops.

Forrest still casts a long shadow in Tennessee. In 2017, his statue was removed from a Memphis park that bore his name. In 2021, his remains and those of his wife were moved from under the marble base at the park to the National Confederate Museum, over 200 miles away.[67] The city where King was lost could no longer venerate Forrest.

The boat ramp by the sunflower field at Fort Pillow is quiet and unmarked today. Yet, faintly, there are voices.

vii. The Crossing of the Trails (Kentucky)

It was my own fault. The tune in my head as I crossed the border into Kentucky was Elvis's "Kentucky Rain." Then it did, for the next two days.

In May of 2015, I had been following the Tennessee River north, a natural route for both steamboats and freedom seekers in the antebellum South of the 1830s. The country is hilly and wooded, perhaps more remote now than it was then. This part of the ride was among the most insular, and now I was riding alone. Rick had turned east for Nashville and a flight home. After he left, I scarcely spoke to another person for two days. Where the Tennessee and Cumberland Rivers approach each other, both are dammed, and they frame the Land Between the Lakes Recreation Area. It's on the scale of a national park. A large stretch of this day was a wet ride through the forest primeval. I did my best to dry off my gear in a motel in Grand Rivers.

The next day dawned unseasonably raw. A big cold wind was blowing down from Canada, spitting rain. Stepping out of the motel, the choice was either spin the wheels or get cold, and sometimes both. This part of western Kentucky remains sparsely settled. The day's ride consisted of fifty miles of hills with a couple of towns and no restaurants. Convenience store pizza would be the cuisine, hopefully with a table to get out of the weather. I approached where the Tennessee and Cumberland empty into the Ohio River, the great boundary between free and slave states before the Civil War. For the next week I would wander between Kentucky on the south shore and Illinois, Indiana, and Ohio on the north. I was entering the Borderland. During the 1830s, it was a place where slave hunters prowled both sides of the river. Bounties were generous, and freedom seekers could trust no one, regardless of race.

At the end of a street in Smithland, Kentucky, next to a flag snapping in the wind, was a stop sign. Someone must have had a sense of humor. Beyond the stop sign was the Ohio River, over a mile across. A dam was in the distance, and wind rows streaked the surface of the water. I imagined a scene from the antebellum era. What freedom seekers would have struggled to reach would suddenly become a very real and daunting thing. It's a big, big river, and something closer to freedom was on the other side. Finding a way across would not be easy.

The dock holds yet another memory. Seth Concklin, the Philadelphia abolitionist who brought Peter Still's wife and children out of slavery in Alabama only to be captured in Indiana, met his end here. His body, still shackled, was found in the Ohio River at Smithland.

Back on the bike, I clawed my way out of one hollow and down into the next, over and over. This was the day with the most climbing, from Mississippi to Lake Erie. I generated huge amounts of heat under the rain gear. The rain had backed off by the time I reached the aptly named hamlet of Joy, Kentucky.

At the crest of one of dozens of nondescript Kentucky hills, a brown sign came into view with writing like hieroglyphics across the top. In Cherokee, the sign marks a site along Nunahi-duna-dlo-hilu-I, or The Trail Where They Cried. I had stumbled upon the crossing of the Trail of Tears and the Underground Railroad. The place is known as Mantle Rock. It has the feel of holy ground. Mantle Rock is the largest freestanding arch east of the Mississippi River.

In December of 1838, freedom seekers were likely in the area. They knew that one way to cross the Ohio without a boat is to hop across from one ice floe to the next. What a freedom seeker would have seen peering out of the forest in that cold December was an amazing sight. I had the sense of ghosts watching ghosts. He or she would have gazed on a great ragtag wagon train stretching to the horizon. This was the detachment of 1,766 Cherokee led by Peter Hildebrand, the last to leave their homeland in Georgia and Tennessee and the largest party on the Trail of Tears.

The river ice that might have been an aid to a single freedom seeker trying to reach the opposite shore was deadly for the huge party of wagons. In late December, the Hildebrand Detachment stopped at Mantle Rock for two weeks, waiting for the Ohio to thaw and become passable for a ferry. Exhausted by the journey and staying near supplies and wagons on the road, it's unlikely many of them visited the great arch itself. Many fell victim to exposure here. It was one of the darkest points of an American tragedy.

Andrew Jackson never traveled along the Trail of Tears, but he was instrumental in how it came to be. Gaunt and strong-willed, he is one of the most revered and reviled figures in American history. He became the personification of the American frontier ethic and of the rejection of the Eastern and Virginia elites that had ruled the country until his presidency. His spare frame, at six-foot-two and 145 pounds, was marked by a life of battles. A British sword had left a scar on his head, rendered at age fourteen. A bullet from a backwoods duel remained lodged in his chest until his death, leaving him in near-constant pain. His victory over the British in the 1815 Battle of New Orleans cemented his fame. Jackson went on to make his fortune in land trading. He was instrumental in the rapid expansion of the cotton and sugar economy of the developing Southeast, driven by the institution of slavery. In that expansion, the Cherokee and the other tribes of the Southeast were simply in the way.

But for the Cherokee in particular, it might be puzzling that he would become their principal antagonist, given the perspective of the earlier part of Jackson's career. In 1814, Jackson led a force of frontier militia against a rebellious group of Creeks known as the Red Sticks. On this expedition, the Cherokee were his allies, thinking it better to fight with the whites than against them. The force cornered the Red Sticks in a meander of the Tallapoosa River known as Horseshoe Bend. The attack of the Cherokee Regiment on the rear of the Red Stick encampment led to the breaching of their fortifications. What followed was a massacre, with 350 women and children taken prisoner but only three men.[68]

Fighting with the Cherokee Regiment that day was their future chief, John Ross. Black-haired and of slight build, Ross was the son of a Scottish trader and a woman of Cherokee and European heritage.[69] He was raised among the Cherokee but could pass as white. Thoughtful, literate, careful with his language, and willing to do what was necessary to survive, John Ross was a formidable leader for a people dealt a bad hand.

Ross and the Cherokee developed courts, a legislature, and a constitution. The 85-character written syllabary that they invented was the language of the writing I had seen on the sign in Kentucky. From their capital at New Echota, they published a bilingual newspaper, the *Cherokee Phoenix*, that was part of the burgeoning media explosion of the day. Obsession with the media is not a new phenomenon among America's chief executives. Andrew Jackson subscribed to as many as seventeen newspapers during the 1820s. When he became president in 1828, his attorney general advised him to take away the Cherokee printing press. It would ultimately be destroyed.

The Cherokee land consisted of parts of modern-day Tennessee, North Carolina, Georgia, and Alabama. Many of the Cherokee pursued an agrarian lifestyle, often including slavery. Ross knew that chances for survival of the Cherokee Nation in the East lay with accommodation. In a letter telling federal commissioners that the Cherokees would not sell land, he closed with: "With great respect, we are politically your friends and brethren."[70]

John Ross became skilled in the ways of Washington as well. As a member of the 1816 Cherokee delegation to the capital, he had the best English of the group and proved adept at pleading the Cherokee case for keeping their lands. Much of Washington was still a blackened ruin following its burning by the British two years before. In their travels around the rebuilding city, the Cherokees made quite an impression. The *National Intelligencer* wrote:

These Indians are men of cultivated understandings . . .
[They] were nearly all officers of the Cherokee forces which
served under General Jackson during the late war, and have
distinguished themselves as well by their bravery as their
attachment to the United States.[71]

But the drumbeat for the removal of Native Americans grew as
white settlement in the Southeast grew. Encroachment on Cherokee
land steadily grew, with little or no enforcement of Cherokee property rights by state authorities. The most prominent advocate for the
policy of moving the Southeast tribes west of the Mississippi came to
the presidency with Andrew Jackson's inauguration in 1829. Jackson
pushed through the Indian Removal Act the following year, making
it the official policy of the nation.

The institution of slavery and the removal of Native Americans
were two sides of the same coin, the same great forces that brought
the Underground Railroad into being. The explosive growth of cotton
made land in the Southeast extraordinarily valuable. This was the land
of the Cherokee and the Creeks, the Chickasaw and the Choctaw. They
needed to be moved for the cotton industry to thrive. The institution
of slavery would provide the necessary labor.

The displacement of Native people did not lack for eloquent opposition. Henry Clay of Kentucky and Daniel Webster of Massachusetts
spoke out in the Senate against removal. Yet one of the most powerful
voices was long anonymous. In an era when women were expected
to play no part in politics, a Hartford schoolteacher by the name of
Catharine Beecher organized the nation's first mass political action
by women. Keeping her identity secret, she organized a letter-writing
campaign against the removal of Native Americans, first among
Hartford women, then among women across the country. Their 1829

Circular Addressed to the Benevolent Ladies of the United States brought petitions with thousands of signatures to the floor of the House of Representatives. Their efforts would narrowly fail. But if the Beecher name sounds familiar, Catharine's younger sister Harriet would write her name in American history as the author of *Uncle Tom's Cabin*. Some of the most prominent abolitionists also fought against these removals. I would see more of the Beecher family further up the Ohio River.

The battle for the Cherokee homeland was far from over. After the passage of the Indian Removal Act, John Ross's supporters in Congress urged him to bring his case before the federal courts. In May of 1830, Chief Justice John Marshall made clear in a letter to a senator that he would listen if a proper case were brought before the Supreme Court. This was not a trifling matter. John Marshall, at seventy-six, had begun as a junior officer in George Washington's army and remained the lion of the Court. Yet the first case failed. In the 1831 case *Cherokee Nation v. Georgia*, the majority, led by Marshall, rejected the argument that the Cherokees constituted a foreign nation. Ross detected in the opinion that Marshall remained sympathetic to the merits of the case, disagreeing only on the standing of the plaintiff.

Ross found a man with such standing. In 1831 Samuel Worcester, a missionary to the Cherokee Nation, was arrested by the Georgia Guard and charged with violating a Georgia law decreeing that no white person should live on Cherokee land without a permit from the state. Here was a case tailor-made for Marshall's court. In the 1832 decision *Worcester v. Georgia*, the Supreme Court issued a ruling blocking Georgia from extending its laws over the Cherokees. Not only could Georgia not incarcerate Samuel Worcester, but it could not use its laws to void the Cherokee constitution or, more importantly, evict the Cherokee. Marshall's majority opinion trenchantly stated that even if the Cherokees had placed themselves under the protection of the United States, "protection does not imply the destruction of the protected."

There was rejoicing in the Cherokee Nation over the Court's decision, but the celebration proved to be premature. As weeks went on, the legal victory proved hollow. Samuel Worcester was not released from prison. The Georgia section of the Cherokee lands was increasingly overrun with surveyors. The Georgia law voiding their constitution went unchallenged. Quite simply, Andrew Jackson and his government ignored the ruling.

Some 125 years later, another war hero, Dwight Eisenhower, would send federal troops to Little Rock, Arkansas, to enforce the Supreme Court's *Brown v. Board of Education* desegregation decision. But Native American removal was Jackson's passionate issue. A political enemy of Jackson reported that he had said, "Justice Marshall has made his decision; now let him enforce it." Whether Jackson in fact said this, his actions fell exactly along those lines. For Eisenhower, the decision to enforce led to one of the seminal moments in the Civil Rights Movement. For Jackson, the decision not to enforce led to the Trail of Tears.

The gears of government turned slowly but relentlessly toward removal. As a last chance, John Ross led one more delegation to Washington in 1838. He carried a petition from over 15,000 Cherokees, with many of the signatures written in the Cherokee syllabary. It was not enough. Under orders from President Martin Van Buren, Jackson's vice president and designated successor, federal troops under General Winfield Scott were sent to remove the Cherokee to "Indian Territory" in the present state of Oklahoma.

Valley by valley and farm by farm, the Cherokee were rounded up from their homes. Ross returned from Washington to find his home occupied by squatters. The Cherokee had been marched off to what today would be called concentration camps. Predictably, crowding and poor sanitation led disease to rip through the camps. The Georgia Guard had followed the advice of Jackson's attorney general. They destroyed the printing press for the *Cherokee Phoenix*. Archaeologists years later would find fifteen hundred pieces of old type.

Many of the Cherokee were forcibly placed on riverboats for the trip west. Chaotic scenes played out on the banks of the Tennessee River. Ross was able to intervene and take charge of the emigration. Wagons and supplies were obtained, and the Cherokee Nation was broken into separate trains or "detachments" for the overland journey. The detachment led by Peter Hildebrand was the largest and the last to leave. A yellowed handwritten roster of Hildebrand's detachment appears on the Cherokee Registry website. John Ross reported to General Scott in November 1838:

> I reached Blythe's ferry on Sunday evening last, and found the great body of Mr. Hildebrand's detachment of Emigrating Cherokees quietly encamped on the South bank of the Tennessee river, and a portion with about twelve wagons, who had crossed, on the north bank . . . At the close of the day about sixty-one wagons of the detachment with the people were safely lodged across the river. The business of crossing was again resumed early this morning, and before 12 o'clock eighteen wagons, carriages . . . with all the people were over.

The seeming orderliness of the procession would not last. Hildebrand's detachment took roughly a month to reach the Ohio River, with winter bearing down on them. A contemporary account describes the scene in Kentucky:

The forward part of the train we found just pitching their tents for the night . . . We found the road literally filled with the procession for about three miles in length. The sick and feeble were carried in waggons. A great many ride on horseback and multitudes go on foot—even aged females, apparently nearly ready to drop into the grave, were traveling with heavy burdens attached to the back—on sometimes muddy streets, with no covering for the feet except what nature had given them.[72]

With floating ice blocking the ferry across the Ohio, Hildebrand's detachment came to rest at Mantle Rock. No written journals were kept, but later in the nineteenth century the ethnographer James Mooney lived among the Cherokee in Oklahoma. Recollections were still vivid:

In talking with old men and women at Tahlequah, the author found that the lapse of over half a century had not sufficed to wipe out the memory of the miseries of that halt beside the frozen river, with hundreds of sick and dying penned up in wagons or stretched upon the ground, with only a blanket overhead to keep out the January blast.[73]

No one knows how many were lost on the Trail of Tears. A modern study estimates as many as eight thousand.[74] Today the Trail of Tears is a National Historic Trail administered by the Park Service. The Cherokee commemorate the trail with a 950-mile bike tour from their land in Oklahoma to their original homeland in Georgia. On the Cherokee website is a photograph of riders at Mantle Rock with their distinctive Remember the Removal jerseys. The background to the shirt consists of some of the faded signatures from the petition that John Ross carried to Washington in 1838.

It occurred to me that most of my journeys were on the trail of people in bondage or in flight. The westbound detachments of the Cherokee were not so different from the southbound slave coffles bound for the land from which the Cherokee had been removed. Though the Cherokee were not chained, there was no less doubt about their destination. The same Kentucky pathways of the Trail of Tears were crossed, silently and simultaneously, by people seeking a life away from slavery. Even to this day, the immigrants in the Vive shelter in Buffalo are part of their own Underground Railroad.

There were miles to go before my own day's journey was over. At the end of the afternoon, I took the ferry across the Ohio to Cave-in-Rock, Illinois. The gray morning had morphed into the gentle season of May, with the cold rains subsiding. My crossing of the great river was uneventful. The town gets its name from a giant cave along the river, once a hideout for pirates and now home to hundreds of swallows fanning out over the water. As I watched the sunset from a hillside above the river, a tug and barge pushed east against the current. In the distance was the dark Kentucky shore, site of one of our nation's lowest ebbs.

viii. Casablanca in a Barber Shop (Kentucky, Indiana)

I paused on the crest of a hill leading down into Madison, Indiana. I'd pushed hard all day to outrun what was sweeping across the land behind me. Earlier that afternoon, I'd checked the Doppler radar. The ladies of the sky were dressed up in their finest orange and red, marching in a line from the west. Now overhead was a black, crackling squall line. I wasn't going to make it. The first drops splatted on the pavement as I stopped along the road to throw on bright yellow rain gear and cut on my front and rear lights. My thoughts briefly flashed to a few weeks earlier in the Mississippi Delta, when Rick and I heard an old Robert Johnson blues tune: "Hellhound on My Trail."

The storm exploded as I flew down the hill into town, spray coming off the front wheel. My fogged and streaked glasses were useless, so I tucked them into my jersey and squinted. My Scylla and Charybdis were the storm drains and streams on the right and the semis and pickups on the left. Hands tight on the bars, I concentrated on holding a line on the shoulder and staying aware of traffic, knowing that a cyclist was the last thing a driver was going to expect.

I stumbled into a coffee shop in downtown Madison thoroughly drenched, peeling off my rain jacket and trying not to make too big of a puddle. A few minutes later, I had my nose in the phone when I heard a voice behind me: "Howdy stranger." There was Tom Pritchard: tall, angular, blue eyes, gray hair and mustache, easy smile. That afternoon in Madison, it had been better than a week since I'd seen a familiar face. Tom had offered me a place to stay four years before as I was riding west to the Pacific. After hosting me for a couple of days, he dropped me back a mile farther up the road than where he'd picked me up. This became the Missing Mile, the only piece of the road from Delaware to Oregon that I didn't ride. We'd corresponded over the years, and I promised I'd try to catch up with him.

Five days before, in Cave-in-Rock and the pirates' lair in Illinois, I'd watched the tugs and barges on the Ohio River in the gathering dusk, seeing barely any lights on the far side in Kentucky. The next morning I took the ferry back across to the Bluegrass State. In the years before the Civil War, the Ohio River formed the boundary between the free states of Illinois, Indiana, and Ohio and the slave state of Kentucky.

Back then slave-hunting gangs roamed both sides of the river. Freedom seekers would rejoice at the sight of the great river but then find themselves in enhanced danger, for they were most exposed along the river trying to make their crossing. For the next 306 miles to Madison, I would be riding in the no-mans-land of the Underground Railroad, what Black Underground Railroad conductor John Parker referred to as the Borderland.

Bicycle route through the Ohio River Borderland, from Smithland, Kentucky to Ripley, Ohio.

The Kentucky side was hard country for cycling. Trying to stay off main roads, I dropped into deep, forested, isolated hollows without cell coverage, often convinced that I was lost. The descents were followed by knee-killing climbs, many of which were too steep to ride. I'd end up pushing the loaded bike up the grade. Towns were rare, and I came to wince at the convenience store burrito. The heat was coming on in late May, and sometimes I would settle into my motel room at night unable to tell if I was hot or cold, a sign of dehydration. If I wasn't careful with water and electrolytes during the day, cramps would grab me like a vise at night the first time I bent my leg the wrong way.

In the midst of all the Kentucky hills, I passed just across the river from Rockport, Indiana. In 1828, a nineteen-year-old Abraham Lincoln and his partner Allen Gentry pushed their flatboat out into the current there with a cargo of barrel pork, bound for New Orleans, 1,276 miles and a world away. I had completed Lincoln's journey to the north.

Kentucky was not without its blessings. One afternoon in the full heat, I was working my way up a steep grade called Folsom Ridge, hugging guardrails on a microscopic shoulder. I didn't make it very far before getting off the bike again to push. I was completely drenched in sweat approaching the crest. As I dismounted to drink from my water bottle, a voice came from a house along the road: "Want to top that off?" I did.

David was the pastor of the Vine Run Church about halfway up the hill. Clean-shaven, clear-eyed, and earnest, he invited me into his air-conditioned house and watched me put away a bottle of ice water in about thirty seconds.

His wife said, "Be careful. There are some crazy people out there."

"I know." I nodded. "I'm one of 'em."

"Can we get you some lunch or snacks? We've got plenty in the kitchen," she said.

"That's very generous," I said. "But I hadn't counted on pushing up all these hills, and it's slowed me up a bit. I still have a long way to go before I can rest my head tonight."

"Where are you bound?"

"Well, I'm on an Underground Railroad route. But ultimately I'm headed for my daughter Laura in Toronto."

David nodded. "Then would you mind if we say a prayer for you?" They each took a hand. "Lord, we pray for this man's safe journey to Canada and to his daughter. Let the road be kind to him, and may you guide him on his way. In the name of Christ our Lord."

I'm not especially religious, and I was fairly confident that I would make it to my destination that night without intervention from David or the Almighty. But there was a warm magic about the house on Folsom Ridge. I'd take all the help I could get.

After banging through the hills of Kentucky and crossing the river into Indiana, I was ready for a rest day in Madison with Tom Pritchard and his wife, Karen. Tom's one of those people who are the heart and soul of a small town. Now retired from a career as an engineer, he took me to the firehouse to show me the pump truck he drove as a volunteer firefighter. Driving into town, he pointed out the new piece of guardrail on Hanging Rock Hill.

"There was just a hole there when the car missed the turn and went through the rail on a rainy night," he said. "We got him out of there. Still can't believe he survived."

Tom was the rough downtown boy who'd won the heart of Karen, the beautiful Hilltop girl, some forty years before. I buried myself in one of Karen's quilts that night, shaking off the chill of the storm.

On this visit, Tom had met me in the downtown historic district of Madison, spread out along the river. Cafes, gift shops, and art galleries in old brick buildings line the main street. Geography defines the town, much as it did in the days of the Underground Railroad. Up on the ridge lies Hilltop, domain of big box stores, fast food restaurants, and the high school. Once upon a time, safety lay there also. While freedom seekers could pause in Georgetown, the free Black community in Madison, the uphill towns of Lancaster and Ryker's Ridge had a long-standing abolitionist society and offered more sanctuary than the turbulent borderland by the river.

The next morning Tom drove me around the Madison area, looking for Underground Railroad sites. Our first stop was the Georgetown neighborhood, a place of intrigue in the antebellum era. Free Black people, many from Virginia, settled the area as early as 1820, and it became a center for Underground Railroad activity, as well as the focal point for the Kentucky mobs attempting to break up the community.[75] Many of the original buildings survive to this day. We stopped by the African Methodist Episcopal Church, built in 1850 when the other Methodist church in town asked members to stop their abolitionist efforts.[76] Down the street was the home of blacksmith Elijah Anderson, referred to as the "general superintendent" of Madison's Underground Railroad. Georgetown was also home to the town barber with a twinkle in his eye: George DeBaptiste.

The Madison of the Underground Railroad era was prosperous, the second biggest town in Indiana. The major industry was pork, what Abraham Lincoln carried down the river to New Orleans. The acrid smells of slaughterhouses and tanneries wafted along the bustling waterfront. Steamboats plied the river, while littering the banks were dozens of flimsy skiffs, often little more than a few planks hammered together.

Across the river, a major industry of Kentucky was the export of human beings. The number of enslavers was relatively small, and the climate didn't support the cotton economy of the Deep South. Instead, Kentucky became known as a "breeding state," the origin of the phrase "sold down the river."[77] Louisville became a port of origin for the enslaved, exporting 2,500–4,000 men, women, and children annually during the 1850s.[78] Lexington was the biggest slave trading market, where the young Peter Still was sold and where his great-great-granddaughter Valerie would have a Hall of Fame basketball career at the University of Kentucky (chapter 2.v). The river that was crucial for the slave trade was also central to how the enslaved might escape. By night those skiffs littering the banks at Madison would be pressed into service for a different kind of traffic.

Into the busy and—for a Black man—intimidating world of Madison stepped George DeBaptiste. His life speaks to his ambition and energy. Born free in Virginia, DeBaptiste had trained as a barber but was soon on the road as the servant of a professional gambler, traveling widely across the country, including the Deep South.[79] After coming to Madison in 1837, he ran a wholesale shipping business going from Madison to Cincinnati. In Ohio, he met future president William Henry Harrison, who later hired him as steward at the White House. DeBaptiste's time in the bright lights would be brief; Harrison died just thirty-one days after his inauguration. DeBaptiste returned to Madison and ran a barbershop for the next six years. But it was far more than a barbershop. A good sense of his side job comes from the memoirs of John Tibbits, a white abolitionist up on the hill in Lancaster:

> I received word from George DeBaptiste of Madison, Indiana, that there would be a lot of ten to leave Hunter's Bottom on Sunday night and he wished me to make arrangements to transport them on the underground road that I was acquainted with. After dark I drove to the place agreed upon to meet in a piece of woods one mile from the town of Wirt. I had been at the appointed place but a very short time when Mr. DeBaptiste sang out, "Here is $10,000 from Hunter's Bottom tonight." A good Negro at that time would fetch from $1,000 up. We loaded them

in, drew down the curtains and started with the cargo of human charges towards the North Star.[80]

Madison was the hub of many Underground Railroad routes, and in the early 1840s, DeBaptiste's barbershop was the nerve center. He gathered information from his contacts in Kentucky about potential freedom seekers across the river and, by night, went down to the riverbank to listen for the sound of muffled oars. By his count, he helped over 180 of the formerly enslaved reach freedom.

But danger was always close at hand. In Georgetown, Tom showed me the site of the stables of sheriff Right Rea, who was the most notorious slave hunter on the Indiana side. Rea would often stake out known Underground routes at night, and he was known to pursue freedom seekers as far north as Michigan. In 1846, a mob of Kentucky enslavers, with Rea's support, invaded Georgetown, bursting into the homes of Black residents and beating those who dared to resist.[81] Fearing for his life, DeBaptiste moved north to Detroit, while Elijah Anderson moved upriver to Lawrenceburg.

After Georgetown, Tom drove me to one of his favorite cycling routes, a narrow little streambed climbing up from the river called Eagle Hollow. To avoid the gangs, conductors used many routes up from the river, and this was one of them. Tom's cycling experience pointed to why this terrain was a favorite on the Underground Railroad.

"You know, on our rides around town, I always think of Eagle Hollow as this tough little grade on our circuit rides, this steady 500-foot ascent that would get the blood pumping," Tom told me. "But day-to-day, we forget about all the history of this place."

Chapman Harris, both a minister and a blacksmith, was a giant of a man and the lead conductor in Eagle Hollow. He stayed on in Madison after the riots had chased DeBaptiste and Anderson from Georgetown. From the more secluded hollow, Harris would beat on an iron bar wedged high in a tree on the river's edge as an all-clear signal. The sound rang clear to the Kentucky side.

Up from the river, Tom and I arrived at the small community of Lancaster, originally settled by Baptists from New England in the early 1800s. The settlers brought their New England ideas with them, forming the Neil's Creek Anti-Slavery Society. The town became a waystation for many of the Kentucky freedom seekers. We walked through the grass to look at a great three-story stone building. It's all that remains of Eleutherian College, founded in 1848 as an interracial school by members of the Society. Eleutheros derives from the Greek adjective meaning "free." The school closed in 1937 but is a National Historic Landmark today.

Tom Pritchard and the former classroom building of Eleutherian College, a National Historic Landmark in Lancaster, Indiana.

George DeBaptiste was run out of Madison, but he wasn't the kind of man to stay down. In Detroit, he not only resumed his career as a barber, but he also worked as a salesclerk, bought a bakery, and eventually bought a steamship. Black men were not allowed to captain ships, so he hired a white man to pilot and ferry cargo—including freedom seekers—across the Detroit River to Canada. He helped form the Colored Vigilant Committee that ran the Underground Railroad in Detroit. Once the Civil War began, he recruited for the regiment that became the 102nd US Colored Troops.[82] One of our better images of DeBaptiste is a statue, pointing across the river to Canada from the Detroit waterfront.

George DeBaptiste is the model for the conductor on the left at the International Memorial to the Underground Railroad on the Detroit River.

Elijah Anderson was not as fortunate as DeBaptiste. Like Harriet Tubman, he dared to venture into the slave states. The "superintendent" of Madison's Underground Railroad made numerous forays into Kentucky to organize and lead escapes of the enslaved both before and after he was run out of town. In 1857 he was captured, convicted, and sent to the Kentucky penitentiary at Frankfort. He was found dead in his cell, probably murdered, on the day he was to be released.

As I was leaving Tom and Karen's that day in 2015, I could sense that they might not be staying in Madison. Their son had moved out to Seattle and was raising a family there. "The kids are growing up without us," Karen said. I talked with Tom recently at their new place outside of Seattle. He was happy, but just a little wistful. His roots would always be small-town Indiana.

The last time I saw Madison was on a foggy morning the day I left Tom and Karen's. I dawdled for one more cup of coffee in town, postponing the ride up to the bridge over the Ohio River and back to the dark shore of Kentucky. I stopped at the midpoint of the span to look back on the town. I could hear a tug's whistle from downriver. In the mist it was easy to imagine the Madison waterfront of 180 years ago, stevedores rolling barrels of pork onto steamboats tied up to the docks. And, pushed up on shore, a fleet of skiffs, waiting for nightfall and their silent passengers.

ix. The Heroes of Ripley (Ohio)

In the town of Ripley, Ohio, back when the Underground Railroad was operating, there lived a preacher up on the hill and a blacksmith down by the river. I had heard about the man on the hill, the hawk-nosed Presbyterian minister who hung a lantern in his window, and I'd come to town to learn about him. But the Black man down by the river who ran the foundry—well, he belongs as a comic book superhero.

I descended the bridge from Madison once again into the Bluegrass State, bound for Ripley. My route veered away from the Ohio River and into the hills, cutting across the northern nub of the state that sticks up near Cincinnati. I paid dearly for that shortcut. As I lay down in bed on my Kentucky nights, my eyes were raw from the sweat that had gotten in them, banging up grade after grade. One climb even had its own sign—"Ganny and Pa's Hill." Cute, but it was one more stinker. (See Ohio River map, on page 184.)

My little motivational motto was "ten [miles] by nine [o'clock]." The reward for such industry was a second breakfast, should the opportunity arise. So it was that an oasis appeared out of the morning mist: in Falmouth, by the South Fork of the Licking River, rose a McDonald's. Across adjacent tables, I shared a few sea stories with an older man in a USS *Essex* ball cap. I casually dropped into the conversation that I was almost a thousand miles from my start in Mississippi. As I was getting ready to ride out of the parking lot, a car pulled up and the window rolled down. My breakfast companion had two twenties in his hand.

"Thank you, that's very kind," I said. "I don't need it. I'm not doing this for a charity benefit. I'm fine."

"A gift from the navy," he said.

Kentucky has wonderful people, but I was ready to leave the riding conditions behind. One scene repeated several times a day: *Round a bend. House with a porch. Dog on the porch. Here he comes.* I was getting a little low on pepper spray. I had a particularly large pit bull on me coming out of Dry Ridge until he got well seasoned. I don't know what it is that dogs like about cyclists, whether it's the thigh or the drumstick. I've cycled in thirty-five states, and Kentucky's dogs are the worst. Adding to my grievance list, the state transportation department is both fond of their rumble strips and parsimonious with their shoulders. So I resolved to cut my time in Kentucky short and spend one last night in Augusta.

Augusta is a graceful old town. Federal-style houses line the well-preserved waterfront, and the visitor's center can be found in an old caboose. Singer Rosemary Clooney's house is along the river, and her nephew George graduated from the local high school. Augusta contains fragments of the years before the Civil War, and of the losing battle against the spreading stain of slavery. I walked by a dormitory of the old Augusta College. The institution became the center of the anti-slavery movement in Kentucky and, as a result, the state legislature revoked its charter in 1849, forcing it to close its doors. John Fee, the abolitionist and founder of Berea College, was forced across the river to Ohio by a mob here. Kentucky's largest mass escape of the enslaved ended here in 1848, when forty-two freedom seekers were captured just south of town.[83]

In Augusta, I stayed at an elegant bed and breakfast, the Parkview Inn, a nice change from my notorious standard-free accommodations. It was graduation night at the high school, and the town restaurant was filled with loud celebrating families. My own final evening in Kentucky brought concentrated last-minute research on bourbon.

Sadly, the next morning was bright, clear, and brutal. I reassembled my head and my bike and rolled down to the riverside. The ferry to Ohio had been running there since 1798, and the present tenant was a small four-car operation. As I made my last crossing of the Ohio River, I was accompanied by a stowaway: the fever was just beginning as I stepped into the Buckeye State. It was to be my companion all the way to Pennsylvania.

In an earlier Ohio crossing, in 1844, Calvin Fairbanks, a young seminarian from Oberlin, was on the ferry to Ripley. He noticed a man crossing in a skiff and hailed him.

"Mister, are you a Kentuckian?"

The man replied that he was. Pointing to Ripley, Fairbanks asked, "Well, what kind of place is this?"

"It is a black, dirty, abolition hole, sir."

Fairbanks asked the man to show him the homes of abolitionists. He pointed to a red brick farmhouse on a bluff above the town. "Dr. Rankin occupies the one on the hill."[84]

John Fee was not the only one driven out of Kentucky by proslavery forces. John Rankin was a minister in the eastern part of the state but was quickly disabused of the notion that he could preach to the enslaved. He moved across the river to Ripley, where the local Presbyterian church had invited him to serve as pastor. He would ultimately build the house on the hill, which still stands today, gazing out over the river.

I checked into the bed and breakfast in Ripley but didn't stay long. From the riverside, I climbed the stone staircase up to the ridge above town. The stairs are known as the Hundred Steps to Freedom, and at the summit sits the Rankin House, a National Historic Landmark. I turned to see the same dramatic view of the seven bends of the Ohio that John Rankin had looked upon each night. The flinty-eyed preacher would scan the dark hills across the river for men on horseback and would light the lantern in the window if the passage appeared safe. According to his autobiography, he and his family assisted about two thousand freedom seekers on their way north. The guide inside the Rankin House on this day was an earnest young high school girl with ties to the past. Her great-great-grandfather had been enslaved.

Rev. John Rankin;
The Rankin House, Ripley, Ohio.

The Rankins made it a habit to leave the door unlocked and a fire going at night in case there were visitors. In the small hours one winter evening, Rankin found a Black woman and her baby huddled by the fire trying to dry off. As they fed her and gave her dry clothes, she told her story. She had escaped across the frozen Ohio River, pursued by slave hunters until she ran out on the soft ice. She fell through several times, managing to keep her baby out of the water and using a fence rail that she carried to climb out.[85] Somehow she made it across and up the hundred steps to the Rankin House. Rankin's family helped her—like many others before and after—on her way to Canada.

The woman and her child disappeared into the Underground Railroad but not from history. Rankin later told the story to Calvin Stowe, one of his son's professors at the Lane Seminary in Cincinnati. Listening quietly was Calvin's wife, Harriet. Harriet dubbed her Eliza, and the tale of mother and child on the ice floes would find its way into *Uncle Tom's Cabin*, the best-selling American book of the nineteenth century. In the years before the Civil War, virtually every literate person in the country knew Eliza's story.[86]

Rankin endured attacks at his house by slave-hunting gangs and assaults by mobs during his abolition lectures, but he had one advantage over the Black abolitionists like George DeBaptiste: his race. He had a substantial support network among white abolitionists reaching all the way to New England. And he never had to risk enslavement as a result of his actions. Down the hill in Ripley, however, was a man who did: running the town foundry by day and crossing the river into Kentucky by night was John Parker, whose house also stands today.

Parker was born in Virginia and as a young boy was marched south in a coffle of four hundred. In his autobiography he describes the journey:

It was in June that I began my chainbound journey to Alabama, where I eventually reached. Our journey was long and tiresome. Imagine yourself chained to a long chain to which men, women and children were also attached . . . I was trudging along a trail called a road through the mountains of Virginia. Every flower was in bloom, the wilderness was all about us, green and living. Azaleas and mountain laurels were in full bloom. Every thing seemed to be gay except myself. Picking up a stick, I struck each flowering shrub, taking delight in smashing down particularly those in bloom.[87]

In Alabama, Parker was lucky to avoid the cotton fields and learn the foundry trade. Amazingly, he was able to earn enough money on the side to secure his freedom. Moving north, he settled by the river in the bustling town of Ripley, with the Kentucky shore just across the water. What followed were the tales of a Black superhero. He made repeated forays across the river to lead out groups of the enslaved. Some, like Harriet Tubman, survived such journeys, and others, like Elijah Anderson, did not.

Parker had his close calls. One day his contact across the river told of a party of ten freedom seekers from central Kentucky camped in the woods, lost. His contact led him to the group. Like Tubman, Parker carried a gun less for protection and more to keep his charges in line. He proceeded to lead them through the forest, avoiding roads in the Borderland, which were sure to be patrolled. At the riverbank the baying hounds picked up their scent as they frantically searched for a boat. But the one they found could not fit them all. As they approached the Ohio shore, they watched as lights converged on the two left behind.[88]

In another episode, Parker developed a friendship with an enslaved man and his wife and resolved to help in their escape. But their enslaver became suspicious and insisted that they bring their baby to him each night to sleep in his bedroom in the big house. Late one night, amid creaking floorboards and squeaking hinges, Parker crept past the headboard to where the crib lay. He grabbed the baby and bolted. With bullets flying overhead, he and the couple ran for the river and to the safety of Parker's skiff.

Parker became notorious in Kentucky. So it was not surprising that during one of his expeditions, he read, nailed to a tree: REWARD $1000 FOR JOHN PARKER, DEAD OR ALIVE. Seeing the poster reinforced his caution. He burned his diary of the 440 freedom seekers he had assisted, and he never allowed anyone to take a photograph of him.

After the Civil War, Parker became a successful businessman in Ripley, running his foundry and blacksmith shop. He was one of the few African Americans to hold patents, in his case for agricultural implements. In the 1880s, he began to tell his stories to a Tennessee reporter. He was an old man, perhaps telling tall tales, as we old men do. Some are documented, but Parker never knew the names of many of the people he rescued. But if half of them were true, the Ripley waterfront holds the memory of an American hero.

Trying to ignore my growing fever, I stopped by the John Parker House, just down the street from my bed and breakfast. Dewey Scott, a big, deep-voiced Black man who is the docent and historian there, paced in front of the white fireplace telling some of Parker's stories. I had a particular question for him.

"I've been riding for a while on an Underground Railroad route, staying in motels," I said. "How did people escaping from slavery ever make it to the Ohio without benefit of food or shelter along the way?"

"Many didn't, of course. And many were sheltered in the community along the way," he said. "But one secret was corn."

"Corn?" I asked.

"A mature cornfield provides both food and an almost impenetrable hiding place. Running in midsummer would mean following the maturing corn while traveling north."

As I wandered back to the B&B along the river, I could feel my fever beginning to spike. I wondered how I was going to be in any shape to ride the next day. Betsy and Vic Billingsley, the innkeepers, had to leave for a family graduation that night. Incredibly, they stocked the refrigerator and let me stay the next day on my own.

"Just lock the door when you go," she said.

I was better after a day under their warm quilts. I figured that I could treat flu like I always had: sleep like crazy for a day or two, then just live with it until it goes away. That model worked well for a desk job but less so for sixty miles a day on the road. On the morning after my rest day, I rolled out of the Ripley Borderland and into central Ohio and storm clouds.

x. Josiah's Road (Kentucky, Indiana, Ohio)

I zipped up my foul-weather gear and enjoyed my last few moments of dryness in Ripley. In less than a mile I was climbing up a winding country road out of the Ohio River Valley east of Cincinnati in a steady rain. I quickly felt what the fever had taken out of me: my legs felt like cast iron. I could appreciate the words of another traveler approaching Cincinnati, in 1830, who wrote of "two weeks of exposure to incessant fatigue, anxiety, rain, and chill."[89] There were a few differences though. Josiah Henson had no warm B&B, indeed no shelter of any kind. He was traveling with his wife and three children. And they were being hunted.

Nine days earlier, in Kentucky, I had stumbled on the route of this man, one of the Underground Railroad's most famous travelers. I didn't realize at the time that I would be following his road for a while. I had spent that cool May day powering my bike into a strong wind outside of

Owensboro, not far from the Ohio River. The fields were tinged with the light green of sprouting corn. Up ahead was a weathered historical marker: UNCLE TOM LIVED HERE. Leaning the bike against the marker, catching my breath, I realized that this was the site of the Amos Riley plantation, where Henson was enslaved and where he made his break for freedom in 1830.

Josiah Henson.

In 1849 Henson became something of a celebrity. His autobiography would be widely distributed that year, and later, he would become the model for the title character of Harriet Beecher Stowe's *Uncle Tom's Cabin*, the giant bestseller of the nineteenth century. He was both a traveler and a conductor on the Underground Railroad, returning to Kentucky a number of times after his escape to Canada. In his autobiography, he claimed to have assisted 118 people to freedom in the West, not unlike Harriet Tubman's role in the East. But a piece of his story was closer to home for me. Before his escape from Kentucky, Henson grew up enslaved by Amos's brother Isaac in my hometown of Rockville, Maryland.

After the publication of the book, the character of "Uncle Tom" became a racist stereotype as a character in minstrel shows and films. Unlike Henson and Henson's fictional portrayal in the book, the minstrel show character was servile, submissive, and devious, a trope that lasted through the Jim Crow era. Henson himself cringed at the characterization. "My name is not Tom and never was Tom," he said. "My name is Josiah Henson, always was, always will be."[90]

The real Josiah Henson ventured boldly into the unknown that night in 1830, bringing his family along to deliver them from the likely fate of the New Orleans auction blocks. He is celebrated in museums both in Canada and the United States. In his and my hometown in Maryland, a major east–west thoroughfare is now the Josiah Henson Parkway.

Henson's earliest memories are of Maryland. In his autobiography, he tells of losing his father, at roughly age four:

> [My father's] right ear had been cut off close to his head, and he had received a hundred lashes on his back. He had beaten the overseer for a brutal assault on my mother, and this was his punishment. Furious at such treatment, my father became a different man, and was so morose, disobedient and intractable, that Mr. N. determined to sell him. He accordingly parted with him, not long after, to his son, who lived in Alabama; and neither my mother nor I, ever heard of him again.[91]

Henson grew up aspiring to excel. He wanted to be trusted and productive, and in that way to earn his security. In the early 1800s, the young Henson presented an oxymoron for a white man, being both enslaved and ambitious. He didn't want to get sold off to Alabama like his father, but it was a difficult fate for him to avoid. Coffles, gangs of the enslaved in chains trudging west to Kentucky or south to Georgia and the Mississippi territory, were common features of the American landscape in those days.[92]

Like the coffles and the freedom seekers, I spent a lot of time out in the weather, but I would usually have a chance for shelter. One afternoon, high on a ridge in Kentucky, thunderstorms started to come up like popcorn. I rolled by a family out on their deck having a barbecue, then looked left and noticed that I couldn't see the far pasture anymore. Lightning flashed nearby. A closer look: the rain front was advancing across the field. Seconds remained. I wheeled the bike around as the first drops were splatting.

I yelled to the dad, "Mind if I hole up in your tool shed?"

He yelled back, "C'mon in the house, but better make it quick."

I wasn't quick enough and ended up shaking myself off on the front porch. I had perfected that rain shake by studying our dog. The family welcomed me inside and gave me a cup of coffee. Enos, the dad, was a retired coal miner, and we passed the time as the storm raged with his stories of life down in the earth.

"That's not an easy line of work," I said.

Enos rubbed a stubbly chin. "Well, I managed to get through thirty years well enough. But there are times it can scare you. The mine, it can move like it's something alive. You can hear the whole thing creak. Sometimes they drop parts of the mountain down into the abandoned shafts to take pressure off the active shafts. Yessir, you can feel the vibration in your chest."

"Think I'm just as happy to stay above ground."

Before too long the storm passed, and with a handshake from Enos, I was back out onto the wet and steaming roads.

I was eastbound. One hundred ninety years earlier Henson was west-bound, leaving Maryland for Kentucky. During his time in Rockville, he had become a preacher. In photographs taken late in his life, he is a bearded gospel man with a benevolent expression. He grew up on Isaac Riley's Rockville plantation and rose to become overseer, an unusual role for an African American. Henson noted of those days, "I accounted, with the strictest honesty, for every dollar I received in the sale of the property entrusted to me." But by 1825 Riley was in serious financial trouble. He decided to send the people he had enslaved to his brother in Kentucky to keep them out of the hands of his creditors. In a measure of the trust Isaac must have felt, he chose Henson to take the group west.

Henson left in February with twenty-one others, including his wife and two children, for a nine-hundred-mile journey through a country he knew nothing about.[93] He embarked on the National Road, today's US 40, across western Pennsylvania's accordion ridges, with names like Haystack Mountain, Chalkhill, and Scenery Hill. I've ridden these roads. The ridges aren't high, but they are remarkably steep. The grades can reach 18 percent, about the limit for a semi-truck. For a cyclist they may be the hardest in the country. They would have been even more challenging for a wagon.

Henson's party would have had company in the snow and the mud. The National Road was the main route to the West, to the new land just beginning to be settled. The country was on the move, the enslaved included.

"Did Josiah's charges have to walk in chains?" I asked Shirl Spicer, the museum manager at the Josiah Henson Museum and Park in Rockville.

"It's not likely that they were in chains," she said. "Think about where they were coming from. They had spent their lives on or near the Riley Plantation. They trusted Henson, who was vastly better than any of the white overseers. Though plantation life was hard, it was the only life they knew. A fugitive slave's lot was dangerous, as Henson would find out. They would follow him to Kentucky."

But there would be temptation along the way. They reached Wheeling on the Ohio River, where they sold the wagon and used the proceeds for a boat to take them downriver to Kentucky. Ohio, just across the river, was a free state. Henson writes:

> At Cincinnati especially, the colored people gathered round us, and urged us with much importunity to remain with them and told [his charges that] it was folly to go on. My companions probably had little perception of the nature of the boon that was offered to them, and were willing to do just as I told them, without a wish to judge for themselves. . . . I had promised that man to take his property to Kentucky, and deposit it with his brother; and this, and this only, I resolved to do.[94]

Freeing them, and himself, would be stealing from his enslaver. He was a moral man in an immoral system. He delivered Isaac Riley's "property," including himself, to Amos Riley a few days later.

For Henson, the walls began to close in after a few years in Kentucky. He gradually came to accept that no matter how hardworking and trustworthy and valuable he became, sooner or later he and his family would be split up and sold. Bankruptcies, estate sales, or the simple need to raise some cash were just things that happened, in the 1820s as today. If his enslavers ever had an honest conversation with Henson, they'd say: *It's nothing personal. Just business.* And a large part of Kentucky's business was the buying and selling of people.

At first he tried to buy his freedom using what he'd earned preaching, but Amos Riley doubled the price as soon as Henson got close to raising the money. He was asked to accompany Riley's son down the Ohio and Mississippi to New Orleans. Henson realized the purpose of his journey after several planters came on their boat to inspect him. He avoided being sold only because the son sickened and needed to be taken back home to Kentucky. After the close call in New Orleans, it became obvious to Henson that his sale and that of his family was imminent. Promises made by Amos Riley were worthless.

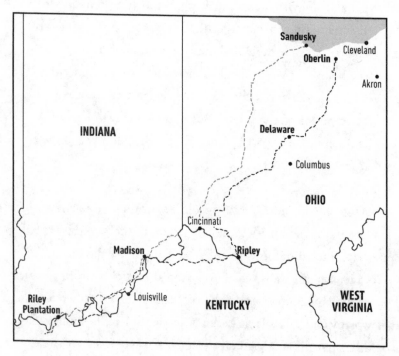

Josiah Henson's route (light dash) and bicycle route (heavy dash).

A moonless night found Henson and his family down by the Ohio River, where a waiting skiff would take them to the Indiana shore. Henson knew better than to believe that reaching a free state would make them free. The only truly safe place for them was Canada, and he resolved to find a way north. His wife had made a knapsack large enough to carry his two youngest sons while the oldest boy walked, and the family traveled as quietly as they could over the 150 miles through Indiana to Cincinnati:

> We were to travel by night, and rest by day, in the woods and bushes. . . . The population was not so numerous as now, nor so well disposed to the slave. We dared look to no one for help.[95]

Trust was a dangerous proposition, since anyone of any race could collect bounties for freedom seekers. Successful slave hunters potentially made $20 to $30 for retrieving a runaway, over $400 in today's dollars. The choice was often between the danger of being betrayed and simple hunger. At one point Henson ventured out on the road in daylight, leaving his family in hiding, and stopped at a house to ask to buy food. The man answered, "I have nothing for n__s!" At a house further up the road, another man answered similarly. Overhearing the conversation, the man's wife replied, "How can you treat any human being so? If a dog was hungry, I would give him something to eat." The man laughed and told her that she might take care of n__s, but he wouldn't. Henson left with bread and venison to take back to his family.[96]

I crossed back into Indiana at Brandenburg, Kentucky, some miles upriver of Henson's escape crossing, and followed his route much of the way to Cincinnati, passing through the river town of Madison (chapter 3.viii). Despite the slave-hunting sheriff, Madison's free Black community was active in helping freedom seekers through the dangerous riverfront town to the inland anti-slavery communities, where they might find shelter. Henson and his family passed through by night, unaware that salvation was at hand.

They made their way along the river to Cincinnati, where they were fed and sheltered, by either abolitionists or people from Cincinnati's large free Black community. After several days, they were carried in a wagon thirty miles north, into western Ohio.

My road to western Ohio was much easier—over the Ohio River into Kentucky at Madison, eastward to Augusta, and back across the river to Ripley (chapter 3.ix). I rode through the gentler terrain of western Ohio on a wonderful network of bike paths, a route that took me east of Henson's road. We both were bound for Lake Erie, and Canada on the other side.

For me, the wet ride north out of Ripley exacerbated my cold. I holed up in a motel in Milford to try to ride out the reemerging fever and see a doctor. The doc ruled out most of the bad guys like bronchitis and pneumonia but advised me to take it easy. Two sleep-filled days in a motel seemed enough. I was anxious to get out onto western Ohio's flat, sweet bike trails now that the weather had cleared. And the next day, I wouldn't be alone anymore.

In the town of Delaware, Jan Kublick once again became my riding companion. As well as following Harriet Tubman's road in New York, we'd ridden together in France and Spain, Montana and Virginia. He was always the better athlete, but usually when he arrived in the middle of rides, I'd have big legs and he'd have some catching up to do. This time, when we met, he sensed that I was hurting.

Near the end of the day out of Delaware, we climbed some steep, nasty little hills. They probably weren't that bad, but with the fever tagging along, they became the Ohio Alps. Halfway up one, I stopped with no legs left, embarrassed by my exhaustion. Amid the smell of road dust and blackberry bushes, I sat down on the shoulder. Just as in the

Tour de France, teammates help each other through the big ascents. Jan was patient. He didn't exactly hook a bungee cord to the back of his bike, but he managed to haul me over the top again and again. Somehow, I got by. In two days we were approaching Oberlin, with Lake Erie not far beyond.

The western Ohio of Henson's day had few settlements. He and his family followed the remnants of a military road, cut during the War of 1812 for the unsuccessful US invasion of Canada. The road had fallen into disrepair, and before long Henson realized that while they were away from slave hunters, they were in the wilderness with little food. Today it's hard for us to imagine wolves in Ohio, but that was what Henson and his family heard.

By late in their second day in the wilderness, they began to notice shadowy figures, probably Shawnee, peering at them from behind trees, then running away. Henson's family approached the intersection of two worlds, neither of which knew anything about the other. They came upon the Shawnee village, where the chief brought the young men out from the woods, and curiosity began to prevail. Henson describes the encounter:

> Each one wanted to touch the children, who were shy as partridges, with their long life in the woods; and as they shrunk away, and uttered a little cry of alarm, the Indian would jump back too, as if he thought they would bite him. However, a little while sufficed to make them understand what we were, and whither we were going, and what we needed.[97]

They took the family in, fed them, and gave them a wigwam for the night's rest. They were now only twenty-five miles from Lake Erie. The Shawnee guided them the rest of the way.

Henson's family would find their own ferry to freedom in the lakeshore town of Sandusky, some two dozen miles west of Oberlin. Coming out of the woods, Henson saw a ship loading cargo along the lake. The foreman asked if he wanted work. After the ship was loaded, Henson revealed his plans to the captain, who agreed to take him across. As always, the question of whether this man could be trusted must have weighed on Henson. It is said that history is written by the winners, but even more so it is written by survivors. How many freedom seekers trusted the wrong person?

Fortunately, Henson's instincts were correct. The captain sent a longboat in from the ship to pick them up after dark, "as there were Kentucky spies, he said, on the watch for slaves . . . To my astonishment, we were welcomed on board, with three hearty cheers." The ship ran down the lake to Buffalo, and the captain paid the family's fare for the passage across to Canada. They reached freedom on the 28th of October 1830. On the Canadian shore, by the torrent that is the Niagara River, rests a marker to where Henson and his family stepped onto free soil.

Freedom was a start, but they had arrived penniless. Henson took a job as a laborer and learned to how to read. Eventually he earned enough to purchase 200 acres in Upper Canada, later known as Ontario. He met Harriet Beecher Stowe in 1849, the same year his book was published. Returning to the United States as a famous man, he could still have been nabbed and returned to the Rileys before the Civil War. Regardless, he made repeated trips back from Canada into Kentucky as a conductor on the Underground Railroad.

Later, as a British citizen of Canada, he visited London and was feted as a celebrity. Twenty-five years after the publication of *Uncle Tom's Cabin*, at age eighty-seven, Henson met Queen Victoria at

Windsor Castle, where he was warmly received.[98] In 1878, he came back to the Riley Plantation in Rockville, where he was once enslaved. At the plantation, now fallen into disrepair, he met Isaac Riley's widow, who, on recognizing him, exclaimed, "Why, Si, you are a gentleman." Henson replied, "I always was, madam."[99]

Josiah Henson never moved back to the United States. He would live out his life in the settlement he founded in Canada for the formerly enslaved. It was called Dawn.

xi. The Magic Shawl (Ohio, West Virginia)

It took a little hunting to find the cenotaph. I even had to look up what a cenotaph was: "A monument to someone buried elsewhere." Jan and I wandered around the town of Oberlin, Ohio, for about a half hour until we came upon a small obelisk tucked away in a local park. Next to it was a plaque, inscribed: THESE COLORED CITIZENS OF OBERLIN, THE HEROIC ASSOCIATES OF THE IMMORTAL JOHN BROWN, GAVE THEIR LIVES FOR THE SLAVE. On the bottom was listed, LEWIS SHERIDAN LEARY, DIED AT HARPERS FERRY, VA., OCTOBER 20, 1859, AGED 24 YEARS. Leary was a member of the famous 1859 John Brown raid on Harpers Ferry, but his brief light would shine into the next century. I would come to follow Lewis Leary around, from the place where he lived, to the place where he died, to the place where he's buried, and even perhaps to the man to whom his spirit was passed.

Approaching Oberlin, Jan and I were both beat up in our own ways. He had joined me in the town of Delaware, Ohio, two days before, and the next day I had heard the ragged sound of bike tires on the gravel shoulder behind me. Jan had gone down, spinning completely around and cracking his helmet. He bounced up quickly, never losing consciousness, and after patching his road rash and procuring a fresh helmet we were riding again.

An hour further on, we came upon a ROAD CLOSED sign. Most closed roads can be traversed on foot, so we rode on to check it out. A bridge was cordoned off with yellow tape. The bridge deck had been removed, exposing about twenty feet of I-beams. Far below, a stream wound through boulders. We tiptoed carefully across the three-inch beams with the bikes on our hips. Jan didn't fall, thus passing his concussion protocol.

I had my own issues. The fever I'd picked up in southern Ohio was proving hard to shake. Rain was forecast for the next day, and the appeal of sleeping in and having breakfast in a coffee shop was irresistible. We were ready for a rest day in Oberlin, a gentle old college town, a place of bookstores and people wandering around in other worlds.

Entering Oberlin, we passed a historical marker on the town square mentioning the cenotaph. A few keystrokes on the smart phone produced an old image. Lewis Leary stared straight out of a scratched daguerreotype: thin mustache, bowtie and jacket, broad-brimmed hat at an angle. A saddlemaker, never enslaved, he had come to town from North Carolina, where his grandfather had fought in the Revolution.

At Oberlin, Leary met up with his nephew, John Copeland. To use today's term, they became radicalized. They both joined the local anti-slavery society, where Leary gave a speech in which he declared, "Men must suffer for a good cause." He traveled to Cleveland and listened to a sparsely attended public lecture by John Brown. In Oberlin, Leary met and married a local African American woman, Mary Patterson.

Lewis Sheridan Leary.

It's no coincidence that Leary and Copeland were drawn to Oberlin. It was probably the most racially progressive town in America, and the college was one of the first higher learning institutions to grant admission to African Americans. Though small in number, Black people in Oberlin bore themselves as though they were not "afraid of the white man. There is sort of a you-touch-me-if-you-dare about them."[100] In the era of the Fugitive Slave Law of 1850 mandating capture and return from anywhere in the country, Oberlin boasted that no freedom seeker was ever returned from its boundaries. That would be tested.

It was my first visit to Oberlin, but not Jan's. He had been here for his stepdaughter's graduation some years back, and he took me around the town on our rest day. We entered the cavernous First Church in Oberlin as a young woman's piano music was echoing through the hall. Here was the pulpit where Ralph Waldo Emerson and Frederick

Douglass, Mark Twain and Martin Luther King Jr. had spoken, and from where the Emancipation Proclamation had been announced. Irresistibly, I was drawn to climb up the steps of the pulpit, put my hands on either side, and look out on where the congregation sat.

Later we went up to the fourth floor of the Oberlin Library, to the archives. When we spoke to the curator of our journey on the Underground Railroad, she looked at us intently, assessing our sincerity. It seems that Jan and I passed.

"We can show you a few things," she said.

She emerged from the back with an envelope and a box, putting on white gloves to open them. In the envelope was a letter, written in a tight, precise hand, from Abraham Lincoln, just prior to his inauguration, to General Winfield Scott, discussing the defenses of Washington. Then she gently opened the box, peeling back layers of silk. At the bottom were rusty leg irons and a neck chain. It was how the archivists care for the shoes at the Holocaust Museum in Washington. And it reminded me of what had started me on this road at the Illinois museum.

We rolled out of Oberlin early the next morning and stopped in Wellington, a pretty little crossroads town about ten miles away. In 1858, a freedom seeker was caught in Oberlin and taken to a Wellington hotel. An abolitionist mob from Oberlin, including John Copeland and Lewis Leary, surrounded the hotel and set the man free. The authorities put thirty-seven from the mob on trial under the Fugitive Slave Law. Newspapers from around the country sent reporters, and it was a case that polarized the nation. Opinion from the South and from many Northern papers saw the rescue as an outrage against property rights and the rule of law. The abolitionist press saw the action as a blow for freedom. Only two from the mob would serve any jail time. On the college campus today is a sculpture of railroad tracks coming out of the ground, celebrating the Underground Railroad. Oberlin remains a town with a courageous old heart.

During this time of leg irons and neck chains, John Brown was quietly soliciting volunteers for his raid at Harpers Ferry, Virginia. Brown was already a famous abolitionist at the time, having gained notoriety from his battles with enslavers in what became known as "Bleeding Kansas." Brown's secret plan was to capture the federal arsenal at Harpers Ferry and to use it as a base for an uprising of the enslaved. Leary and Copeland joined in the effort from Oberlin. In 1858, Brown visited St. Catharines, Ontario, trying without success to recruit Harriet Tubman. The following year Brown traveled to Chambersburg, Pennsylvania, to meet with Frederick Douglass, the most prominent Black abolitionist, along with formerly enslaved Oberlin resident Shields Green. Douglass refused to join the efforts, stating "you're walking into a perfect steel-trap." As Douglass was leaving, he turned to the soft-spoken Green and asked him what he had decided to do. "I believe I'll go with the old man," he replied.[101] Leary, Copeland, Green, and Brown would never return.

Leary left his wife and infant daughter, telling them he was going in search of work. The raiders gradually gathered at a farm outside Harpers Ferry. Brown had a shipment of pikes delivered, to be used by those he hoped would rise up after the taking of the arsenal. Leary carried with him a blanket shawl that belonged to his grandfather.[102]

The fight at Harpers Ferry was desperate and short. Leary and Copeland were assigned, along with John Henry Kagi, to take control of the US Rifle Works on Halls Island, about a half mile from town. They took the Rifle Works that night but quickly found themselves in a perilous situation, as Frederick Douglass had foreseen. Brown's raid had triggered thoughts of the worst nightmare of the South: a slave revolt. Militia poured in from the surrounding countryside. By morning the three men were pinned down inside the Rifle Works. Cut off from the rest of the raiders, they made a break under heavy fire to escape across the shallow Shenandoah River. Kagi was shot and killed immediately. Leary and his cousin Copeland made it to rocks out in the river, but Leary had been hit several times. The two surrendered, and Leary, mortally wounded, was dragged back to the riverbank. He lingered until the next morning.

The rest of the Harpers Ferry story is well known. John Brown and the remnants of his band were surrounded in a fire engine house. US Marines under Colonel Robert E. Lee arrived and later stormed the engine house, killing or capturing the remaining raiders. Brown and the other survivors were tried and executed over the coming months. Copeland and Shields Green were convicted of murder, not treason, since Black people were not considered citizens and could not be found treasonous.

The Harpers Ferry raid remains controversial to this day. Most acknowledge that it hastened the start of the Civil War. The historian Winston Groom contends that John Brown's "murderous" raid helped incite a war that did not have to happen, as slavery would have vanished on its own had it been confined to the South.[103] Yet the idea of slavery's inherent end is based on the notion that it was an inefficient form of labor soon to be weeded out by economic realities. By 1860, this system had been growing for seventy years at a rate unprecedented in human history,[104] and the right to bring the enslaved into the new territories had been granted by the Supreme Court's 1857 Dred Scott decision. The institution of slavery wasn't going anywhere.

A year after the first Underground Railroad ride, I took a day to ride from my house in Maryland to Harpers Ferry on the dusty Chesapeake and Ohio Canal towpath. From there it's a walk on a footbridge over the Potomac River into the old town, now a national historical park. It's a supremely dramatic setting, where the Potomac and Shenandoah

Rivers meet to pour through a gap in the mountains. It is a place, as Langston Hughes put it:[105]

Where the hills of the North
And the hills of the South
Look slow at one another—

I asked at the visitor center how to get to the place where Leary and Copeland and Kagi had made their last stand. The volunteer said, "You need to talk to David Fox. He knows as much about the raid as anyone around here. He's running a tour now, but if you go up by the Point you should run into him."

The Point was the place that Langston Hughes wrote about. Speaking to a crowd of tourists against the backdrop of the hills was an intense park ranger, gray goatee and wire-rimmed glasses. We talked with David Fox on the walk back to the village.

"The Rifle Works is not far at all, maybe a twenty-minute walk. You won't find much there now, but at the time of the raid it was a big factory next to a canal, driven by water power. The raiders didn't have much of a chance by the morning, surrounded on three sides by the militia. Out in the shallow river was their only chance to escape. We don't know exactly where they were caught, or even if the rocks are still there. But that's where Leary and Copeland were."

David Fox drew a map to the site of the Rifle Works. Back in Lewis Leary's day, it was a bustling Industrial Revolution site, described by a tourist as "a most abominable village . . . the smell of coal smoke and the clanking of hammers obtrude themselves on the senses . . ."[106] The Rifle Works would be ravaged by man and nature after that day in 1859. Stonewall Jackson's army would destroy it in the Civil War, and repeated floods of the Shenandoah leveled attempts to build new industry there. I walked to the small cylindrical water turbine pit back in the woods—all that's left of the original factory. From there, I followed the path of the three raiders to the river. Out in the shimmering water was where Copeland and Leary surrendered.

The Shenandoah rocks at Harpers Ferry, where Lewis Leary was killed.

In the aftermath of the Harpers Ferry raid, the treatment of the bodies of the raiders reflected the rage of the surrounding country. Two of the bodies were donated to a local medical school for dissection. Bodies of eight others, including Lewis Leary, would not be accepted at the local cemetery. Instead, they were packed into two boxes and buried in an unmarked grave near the banks of the Shenandoah.

Lewis's journey did not end there. In a town called North Elba, in the Adirondacks of northern New York, John Brown had established a farm for the formerly enslaved and his family ten years before Harpers Ferry, on land purchased by Gerrit Smith. Brown had stated his wish to be interred there, and his wife accompanied the funeral cortege on the long trip north following his 1859 execution. Even this journey was so controversial that a decoy coffin was sent ahead to a local undertaker. But the real coffin made it to North Elba, and Brown received a hero's burial, along with two of his sons. Lewis's remains would wait forty years to join him.

In 1899, Dr. John Featherstonhaugh, a Washington civil servant and president of the Humane Society there, led a group of three men to clandestinely exhume the remains of the eight men at Harpers Ferry. The remains were quickly spirited out of town and brought to the undertaker in North Elba. There the burial attracted far more attention, including a military detachment dispatched by the secretary of state.

I visited John Brown's farm in North Elba at the peak of fall colors on a stone-gray day. It's now a state historic site, just outside busy Lake Placid. The Olympic ski jump looms over the old farmhouse. The Adirondacks are a cold, snowy place, and it's difficult to imagine a harder place to claw a living from the land. Next to a great boulder is where John Brown's body lies, together with twelve of his raiders, including Lewis Leary.

Graves of John Brown, Lewis Leary, and the other
Harpers Ferry raiders, North Elba, New York.

But North Elba was not quite the end of Lewis's road. According to family lore, his blanket shawl was returned from Harpers Ferry to his widow. Mary Patterson Leary remarried and, some years later, came to raise a young grandson, born into the new century. She would wrap the baby in the shawl, perhaps believing in passing on the spirit of the young husband she had known to be "brave to desperation."

The shawl rests today at the Ohio Historical Society in Columbus.[107] When I arranged to see the shawl, I imagined entering a great glass-and-steel museum. Instead I pulled up to a windowless prefab building in an industrial park, the sort of place one would expect to find the remains of Roswell UFOs. I gently rang the doorbell. The steel door swung open and Rebecca Odom, the curator, escorted me to a broad, flat table with a large cardboard tube. She put on latex gloves and gently unrolled "one of the most treasured objects in our collection."

Rebecca Odom and the shawl.

The blanket shawl is a large, tattered piece of brown wool with blue stripes. It has holes from moths and holes from wear along the folds. But if objects can have power, the shawl does. The baby that Mary Patterson wrapped in the shawl grew to be a young vagabond, traveling from city to city, even crewing on a tramp steamer to Africa. He worked as a busboy at a Washington hotel before his poems gained recognition. Langston Hughes would become the great poet of the Harlem Renaissance. He wrote of rivers and jazzmen, of weary blues and dreams deferred.

In his donation of the shawl in 1943, Hughes enclosed a handwritten note: "Sheridan [Lewis] Leary wore this shawl when he went from Oberlin, Ohio, to join John Brown in order to help him create the slave revolt which they hoped might free the Negroes." Some have questioned whether such an artifact could have actually made it back from Harpers Ferry to Oberlin in that turbulent time.[108] Perhaps so. What is sure is that Hughes kept the shawl as something precious, and that Leary was never far from his thoughts. Earlier in his career, he wrote of that place where the Potomac and the Shenandoah come together:

> *Since Harpers Ferry*
> *Is alive with ghosts today,*
> *Immortal raiders*
> *Come again to town—*
> *Perhaps*
> *You will recall*
> *John Brown.*
>
> *October 16: The Raid*

4

Freedom City

Fighting my way through the fever, I rode with Jan through Ohio along the shores of Lake Erie—from Oberlin, around Cleveland, then east to the Pennsylvania line. Jan left in Lake City, a small Pennsylvania town on the lake. We'd had a lot of miles together, on and off the bike, as best men at each other's weddings and godfathers to each other's firstborn. This time, he managed to pull me through the hardest part of the ride.

I wanted to keep going, to make it all the way to Canada like Henson and Tubman had done. But my legs were as heavy as iron. I talked with Concetta every night, and she knew something was up.

"I'm coming to get you," she said. "Find a place for us to meet."

She scraped me up at a B&B in the town of North East and deposited me in a soft bed there under a deep quilt. The next day she drove me to our daughter's apartment in Toronto. After 1,500 miles on the road, I slept for two days while the fever finally burned itself out.

In the years before the Civil War, Toronto had been a resting place for freedom seekers as well. Indeed, it became known as Freedom City. By 1834, slavery had been abolished throughout the British colonies, and Toronto was a burgeoning city where schools, churches, and public institutions were open to every immigrant, regardless of color.[1] Black people in Canada certainly faced racism, among other hardships of the newly arrived, but a return to slavery was not among them. Lezlie Harper, a descendant of 1850s freedom seekers from Kentucky, took us on a tour of Black history sites in Ontario near the US border. As we walked through a Coloured Cemetery, she told of the view of her ancestors, who simply wanted to pursue a normal life: "We's here, we's free, we done."

Lezlie's tour was like American history in a funhouse mirror. Laura Secord is mythologized in Canadian history as the woman who walked twenty miles to warn British troops of an impending American attack during the War of 1812. She is Paul Revere with gender and sides reversed. In the same conflict, the Coloured Corps, a Black militia, helped fight off the Americans at Queenston Heights. Like the US Colored Troops in the US Civil War a half century later, they likely believed, not without reason, that they were fighting for freedom, and that defeat would mean a return to slavery.[2] At a final stop, Lezlie showed us the spot on the turbulent Niagara River where Josiah Henson first set foot in Canada as a free man in 1830, eight years before Frederick Douglass stepped off the ferry to freedom in New York City.

The experience on Lezlie Harper's tour wasn't uncommon on these bike rides. For my two other books, both on climate change, the act of traveling by bicycle allowed the people I met to open up to personal reflection on this often-uncomfortable subject. I was an unthreatening stranger; if I meant them harm, I had the world's slowest getaway car. Then and now, the bike is a story machine. The people I encounter—in diners, in convenience stores, at historical sites—and the tales they tell are what make the ride. On these Underground Railroad rides, the people I met had a passion for the past, for their small-town and big-city heroes, and for what that past means for today. I had the opportunity to hear their stories, often oral histories being passed down and preserved on a personal level. My riding companions and I were learning of these amazing stories and histories for the first time, when it had been "known" to so many in that local area for so long. We had the chance to listen.

In looking back on the rides, whether those I've done for this book or others, I'm often asked if it's dangerous to be out on the road solo, even to the point of questioning whether I carry a gun (I don't). In our age of mass media, we seem to have convinced ourselves that psychopaths lurk around each corner. My experience from cycling is overwhelmingly that of running into kind people who want to help me on my way, whether it's through urban or rural environs, East or West Coast, mountains or prairie. But things were quite different in the days of the Underground Railroad. The hunters were indeed around every corner, and the light of day held danger. The act of gauging whom to trust was constant, and a mistake fatal. Naivete and paranoia are points of view that depend very much on context.

I found that Toni Morrison's "benches by the road" and the tracks of the Underground Railroad often hide in plain sight, or within earshot if you ask and listen. Many lie close to places we know well. On the American side of the river in the town of Niagara Falls, waiters at the Cataract House led dramatic escapes to Canada. Jackson Square, where Leon Waters showed us the hidden history of New Orleans, is the heart of the French Quarter. The Peter Mott House sits off the nearby roar of the New Jersey Turnpike.

Just a few blocks from the Brooklyn Bridge, I stood on a Manhattan street looking into an eyebrow salon, where the front desk attendant gave me an occasional sidelong look. There I was, daydreaming 156 years into the past, imagining Harriet Tubman there, asleep on the floor of the Anti-Slavery Society, waiting for the contributions that would help bring her parents out of slavery.

In harder to reach places, my rides allowed me to conjure people whose names are lost to history. On a cold day, spitting rain, I clawed over the last of a dozen Kentucky hills to roll into the town of Smithland. At the end of a dock, I first laid eyes on the Ohio River, the great boundary, the River Jordan for those seeking freedom. People must have come there after long, fitful journeys by night to gaze on the land beyond, where, if they were not necessarily free, at least slavery was not legal. The first sight of the river must have brought both joy and fear. The Promised Land still lay in the distance, across a great expanse of water. Harriet Beecher Stowe's Eliza and Toni Morrison's Sethe are characters based on Black women who crossed the Ohio on ice floes with their children. How do we conceive of such desperation?

People that carry the light of the Underground Railroad endure. The Still family of New Jersey and Pennsylvania stretches from the Guinean prince to the Women's Basketball Hall of Fame. Paul and Mary Liz Stewart not only restored the Myers Residence in Albany, but they run the Underground Railroad Education Center. In quiet Peterboro, Norman Dann keeps the legacy of Gerrit Smith alive while his wife, Dot Willsey, operates the National Abolition Hall of Fame and Museum there.

The African Methodist Episcopal churches endure. Mother Bethel in Philadelphia opened her doors to us. Star Hill in Delaware gave us the scripture: *Come to me, all you who are weary.* At journey's end, we the weary were embraced by the community at Salem Chapel in St. Catharines, Ontario, where we could hear the echoes of the formerly enslaved people who gathered here to rejoice in their freedom.

I found heroes celebrated along the road, notably Harriet Tubman and Frederick Douglass, names that are known and acclaimed. But far more have gone unremembered. We erect great monuments to freedom fighters who prevailed, but we neglect those who risked everything for freedom and lost: Lewis Leary of Oberlin, Elijah Anderson of Madison, "Big Jack" Jackson of Milliken's Bend. Charles Deslondes and his fellow rebels of the Louisiana River Road are only recently recognized at the Whitney Plantation. There are likely more that were forgotten than we could ever resurrect.

Perhaps we celebrate the heroes of the Underground Railroad because successful escapes were so rare against the background of the massive institution of slavery. In some places, the vestiges of slavery remain. Lynn, Rick, and I took a day ride from our homes in Maryland and Virginia to the Freedom House Museum in Alexandria, Virginia. The museum is on the site of what was the largest slave trading operation in the country, that of Franklin and Armfield. We'd come across the story of Isaac Franklin, the co-owner, before. He ran the Natchez slave trading market at Forks of the Road and owned Angola, the plantation that became the Louisiana state prison. In his Alexandria business, the enslaved were gathered in pens and formed up in coffles either for shipment by sea to the Deep South or for marching the thousand miles by land to Natchez or New Orleans. One particular story caught my eye. Lewis Henry Bailey was sold as a child through the Alexandria pens and enslaved on a Texas plantation. After the Civil War, he walked back from Texas to reunite with his mother. He would found five churches and two schools in northern Virginia.[3]

Freedom House closed a circle for me. The land route from Alexandria has been called "Slavery's Trail of Tears."[4] I have ridden most of that route, down the Shenandoah Valley to Tennessee, and on the Natchez Trace. Many of the people whose chained feet wore the deep cut in the forest on the Trace passed through this place in Alexandria. It has shaped the landscape.

This institution of slavery carries a legacy. As Clint Smith writes in *How the Word Is Passed:*

> The history of slavery is the history of the United States. It was not peripheral to our founding; it was central to it. It is not irrelevant to our contemporary society; it created it. This history is in our soil, it is in our policies, and it must, too, be in our memories.[5]

For white people like me, the memory of slavery has been pushed back, minimized, forgotten, much like the city fathers of Natchez pushed the slave trading operation at Forks of the Road to a site outside the city limits. A rising movement in the present day is about minimizing this memory in our schools and ensuring that white students aren't made uncomfortable. Tennessee law HB 580, passed in 2021, prohibits teaching in which "an individual should feel discomfort, guilt, anguish, or another form of psychological distress solely because of the individual's race or sex." Identical language is found in a Texas law (HB 3969[6]), passed shortly afterward.

White guilt is not the intended outcome of remembering what happened. Rather we need an understanding, an acknowledgment, a coming to terms. There are things in our history that *should* make us uncomfortable. If you're not wriggling in your chair a little bit, you're not listening. I indeed felt "discomfort" on discovering that my namesake was responsible for the loss of 115 enslaved people on a single voyage on the Middle Passage. Only in grappling with the truths of our past can we begin to construct something new and better.

None of the present deliberate amnesia is new. In his 1935 book *Black Reconstruction in America,* W. E. B. Du Bois wrote: "One is astonished in the study of history at the recurrence of the idea that evil must be forgotten, distorted, skimmed over." Bryan Stevenson, founder of the Equal Justice Initiative, puts it this way:

> There is a kind of smog in the air that's created by the history of slavery and lynching and segregation, and I don't think we can get healthy, we can be free until we address this problem. But to get there, we're going to have to be willing to tell the truth . . . I think it's important that we understand all the brutal, all the ugly details because those are the things that might allow us one day to lay claim to something really beautiful.[7]

One stop on the ride, in Albany, helped me to glimpse the beauty that Stevenson wrote about. At the Myers Residence, Paul Stewart wove a story for us about the discovery of the remains of the fourteen enslaved people at Schuyler Flatts and how the people of Albany decided to honor them. That story still reverberates. In 2021, historian Jill Lepore interviewed Cordell Reaves, who was working for the New York State Office of Parks, Recreation and Historic Preservation when he learned about the discovery of the remains. Lepore gives Reaves's account of the reburial over a decade later:

> The dead lay in state in the front hall of Schuyler Mansion before the multi-faith burial, in one of the best attended and most moving public-history events the state has ever hosted. Reaves wept. "It was like lightning struck," he told me. All that night and the next day, people read poems, and sang, and danced. "Something about this captured people," Reaves said, tearing up again. "I'm not sure what it was. But I keep coming back to the word 'reconciliation.'"[8]

I can't pretend to know what reconciliation looks like. But a string of voices through history to today, from Du Bois to Baldwin to Stevenson, tells us that we can't keep reburying our past. National trauma, like a wound, tends to heal when it's exposed to the air. For me, that road began at a rural museum in Illinois.

Maybe part of the answer was in code, up on the wall at the Myers Residence. A tall copper sculpture with African symbols, homage to fourteen lost and rediscovered. Fourteen photos of beautiful, intricate wooden boxes, all deep in the ground now. And the photo of a small Black woman with a huge tattooed white man, both deep in thought next to one of the ossuary boxes. Perhaps I read too much into a moment's image, but something in the photograph speaks to me of grace and hope and reconciliation.

*Dan Hogan, artist and woodworker, and Evelyn King, chair of the
Re-Burial Committee, next to one of the Schuyler Flatts ossuaries.*

Acknowledgments

On my bicycle journeys on the Underground Railroad, I rarely rode alone. My fellow riders spun wheels on sparkling days and suffered rain, headwinds, and bad jokes. Lynn Salvo racks up Guinness Records while riding into her 70s, and it's a privilege that she joined me on the road to Ontario. Rick Sullivan rode with a guitar strapped onto his bike from New Orleans to Tennessee, introducing me to the Delta blues along the way. He also brought the guitar from Maryland to New York. Jan Kublick is my oldest friend, bailing me out of hard times in Ohio and welcoming us to his home turf in Central New York. On occasion we were able to ride pannier-free thanks to support and gear drivers. Sandra West supported us through the Hudson Valley and Central New York, while Concetta Goodrich took over for the rest of the ride to Ontario.

The first of the Underground Railroad rides, from Mississippi to Lake Erie, was based on a route laid out by the Adventure Cycling Association. The southern part of the Harriet Tubman ride from Maryland to Ontario follows the wonderfully detailed Harriet Tubman Underground Railroad Byway, while the northern part drew much information from Charles Blockson's *Hippocene Guide to the Underground Railroad*.

ACKNOWLEDGMENTS

My most important guides on these journeys are two people whom I feel like I know through their books. Fergus Bordewich's Underground Railroad history *Bound for Canaan* was particularly useful for the western rides, while Kate Clifford Larson's biography *Bound for the Promised Land* is the definitive source for Harriet Tubman's life and times. These are probably the most dog-eared volumes on my bookshelf.

The support of my writing group has been essential. Their reviews of these chapters were sometimes hard, often detailed, and always constructive. Thanks go to my friends Sarah Birnbach, Jean Campbell, Sherlyn Goldstein-Askwith, Darci Glass-Royal, Andrea Hansell, Leslie Lewis, and Silvia Spring.

My children, Tom Goodrich, Laura Doering, and Andrew Goodrich, all found ways to support the rides, from a sendoff with a grandson in pajamas in the Bronx to a place to rest and recover in Toronto.

As readers, we don't often appreciate the effort that it takes to turn a manuscript into a book. Stephanie Marshall Ward did a superb, comprehensive copy edit. I constantly flip around for maps when I'm reading, and Lara Andrea Taber once again drafted the maps for my manuscript. Maria Fernandez cared for the volume through design and production.

Finally, I'd like to thank two pilots on my travels through the publishing world. My agent, John Silbersack, has been both generous and thoughtful with his advice, and it's an honor to be on his roster of authors. I'm fortunate that my publisher, Jessica Case, is both a former triathlete and a superb present-day editor, and she's guided me through three books now. She's welcomed me and championed my work at Pegasus.

Image and Poem Credits

All photos by the author unless otherwise noted.

p. 10.   Harriet Tubman mural "Take My Hand" by Michael Rosato, Cambridge, Maryland. Used by permission.

p. 12   Harriet "Minty" Tubman's original runaway advertisement, offering a reward for her capture. Courtesy of Jay and Susan Meredith.

p. 17   Lynn Salvo, Rick Sullivan, and the author. Photo by Concetta Goodrich.

p. 37   Longwood Meeting photograph courtesy of Chester County History Center, West Chester, Pennsylvania.

p. 41   Engraving of William Still courtesy of the William Still Collection, Charles L. Blockson Afro-American Collection, Temple University Libraries, Philadelphia, Pennsylvania.

p. 46   Ben Franklin Bridge. Photo by Lynn Salvo.

p. 61   Paul Stewart. Photo by Lynn Salvo.

p. 64   Courtesy of New York State Museum, Albany, New York.

p. 70   Civil War photographs, 1861–1865, Library of Congress, Prints and Photographs Division. Accessible at https://www.loc .gov/pictures/resource/cwpb.04084/?co=civwar&fbclid=IwAR3k PY8hRsJRjusPV_2D7ly_apCASVQXtqBQ49zdcdOZLzYuy FCJaeOIItA.

p. 75   Daguerreotype of the Anti-Fugitive Slave Law Convention. Courtesy of Madison County Historical Society, Oneida, New York.

p. 88   Valerie O'Hara. Photo by Concetta Goodrich.

p. 93   Down in the weeds. Photo by Lynn Salvo.

p. 96   Lithograph of Niagara Falls Suspension Bridge. Library of Congress Prints and Photographs Division.

p. 102   Lynn Salvo, Rochelle Bush, Harriet Tubman, and the author. Photo by Concetta Goodrich.

IMAGE AND POEM CREDITS

p. 120   Sharon Lavigne. Photo courtesy of The Goldman Environmental Prize.

p. 191   George DeBaptiste statue at the International Memorial to the Underground Railroad on the Detroit River. From Creative Commons.

p. 196   Rev. John Rankin. Library of Congress Prints and Photographs Division.

p. 201   Josiah Henson. Library of Congress Prints and Photographs Division.

p. 213   Lewis Sheridan Leary photo courtesy of Oberlin College Archives.

p. 220   Rebecca Odom and the shawl. Courtesy of the Ohio History Connection.

p. 221   "October 16: The Raid" from *The Collected Poems of Langston Hughes* by Langston Hughes, edited by Arnold Rampersad with David Roessel, Associate Editor, copyright © 1994 by the Estate of Langston Hughes. Used by permission of Alfred A. Knopf, an imprint of the Knopf Doubleday Publishing Group, a division of Penguin Random House LLC. All rights reserved.

p. 229   Dan Hogan and Evelyn King. Photo by Paul Stewart.

Endnotes

A NOTE ON LANGUAGE

1   Underground Railroad Education Center, "The Vocabulary of Freedom," blog post, accessed February 8, 2022, https://undergroundrailroadhistory.org /the-vocabulary-of-freedom/.

2   Nancy Coleman, "Why We're Capitalizing Black," *New York Times*, July 5, 2020, https://www.nytimes.com/2020/07/05/insider/capitalized-black.html.

1. BENCHES BY THE ROAD

1   "The TransAtlantic Slave Trade," Small Island Read 2007, Bristol Public Library, http://www.bristolreads.com/small_island_read/slave_trade.htm.

2   Patricia Jackson, "1790 Letter from John Fowler to James Rogers and Company," Jamaican Family Search Genealogy Research Library, 2013, http://www.jamaicanfamilysearch.com/Samples2/Fowler1790.htm.

3   Public Broadcasting Service, *The African Americans: Many Rivers to Cross,* episode 2, "The Age of Slavery," aired October 29, 2013, available at pbs.org.

4   Clint Smith, *How the Word Is Passed,* (New York: Little, Brown, 2021), 252.

5   Toni Morrison, "A Bench by the Road," *World: Journal of the Unitarian Universalist Association* 3, no. 1 (January/February 1989): 4–5, 37–41.

2. FREEDOM ROAD EAST

1   Kareem Abdul-Jabbar, *Black Profiles of Courage,* (New York: William Morrow and Company, 1996), 92.

2   Kate Clifford Larson, *Bound for the Promised Land: Harriet Tubman, Portrait of an American Hero,* (New York: Random House, 2004), 43.

3   Larson, *Bound for the Promised Land,* 137.

4   Charles Blockson, *Hippocene Guide to the Underground Railroad,* (New York: Hippocene Books, 1994).

5   Michael Ruane, "Harriet Tubman's Lost Maryland Home Found, Archaeologists Say," *Washington Post*, April 20, 2021, https://www.washington post.com/history/2021/04/20/harriet-tubman-maryland-home-found/.

6   Larson, *Bound for the Promised Land*, 56.

7   Frederick Douglass, *Narrative of the Life of Frederick Douglass, an American Slave*. (Boston: Anti-Slavery Office, 1845), 64, https://docsouth.unc.edu/neh /douglass/douglass.html.

8   Larson, *Bound for the Promised Land*, 112.

9   Sarah H. Bradford, *Scenes in the Life of Harriet Tubman* (Auburn, N.Y.: W. J. Moses, 1869), 60, digitized at https://docsouth.unc.edu/neh/bradford /bradford.html.

10 Moises Velasquez-Manoff and Gabriella Demczuk, "As Sea Levels Rise, So Do Ghost Forests," *New York Times*, October 9, 2019, https://www.nytimes .com/interactive/2019/10/08/climate/ghost-forests.html.

11 Roseanne Skirble, "Chronic Flooding Threatens Sites Along Harriet Tubman Underground Railroad Byway," *Maryland Matters*, October 11, 2021, https ://www.marylandmatters.org/2021/10/11/chronic-flooding-threatens-sites -along-harriet-tubman-underground-railroad-byway/.

12 William Still, *The Underground Rail Road*, (Philadelphia: Porter and Coates, 1872), 72–74, digitized at https://www.gutenberg.org/files/15263/15263 -h/15263-h.htm.

13 Larson, *Bound for the Promised Land*, 138–40.

14 Thomas Garrett, letter to Sarah Bradford, in Bradford, *Scenes*, 52.

15 Larson, *Bound for the Promised Land*, 143–44.

16 Larson, *Bound for the Promised Land*, xiii, 129.

17 Eric Foner, *Gateway to Freedom: The Hidden History of the Underground Railroad*, (New York: W. W. Norton and Company, 2015), 155–56.

18 James McGowan, *Station Master on the Underground Railroad: The Life and Letters of Thomas Garrett*, (Moylan, Penn.: Whimsie Press, 1977), 129–31.

19 Bradford, *Scenes*, 51.

20 David W. Blight, *Frederick Douglass: Prophet of Freedom*, (New York: Simon and Schuster, 2018), 71.

21 Bradford, *Scenes*, 30–31.

22 Albert J. Wahl, "The Progressive Friends of Longwood," *Bulletin of Friends Historical Association* 42 (Spring 1953): 122–36, https://www.jstor.org/stable /41944495?seq=1.

23 "The Marlborough Riot," Marlborough Meeting, accessed June 5, 2020, http://www.marlboroughmeeting.org/V2/MarlboroughRiotV2.html. See also Christopher Densmore, "Be Ye Perfect: Slavery and the Origins of the Yearly

Meeting of Progressive Friends in Chester County Pennsylvania," *Quaker History* 92, no. 2 (Fall 2004): 39–40.

24 Susan Phillips and Dana Bate, "Faulty, Old Pipe Caused PES Refinery Explosion, Sending a Bus-Size Piece of Debris Flying across Schuylkill," WHYY, Philadelphia National Public Radio, October 16, 2019, https://whyy .org/articles/faulty-old-pipe-caused-pes-refinery-explosion-sending-a-bus -size-piece-of-debris-flying-across-schuylkill/.

25 Daelin Brown, "Two Years After a Huge Refinery Fire in Philadelphia, a New Day Has Come for Its Long-Suffering Neighbors," *Inside Climate News*, July 2021, https://insideclimatenews.org/news/05072021/two-years-after-a -huge-refinery-fire-in-philadelphia-a-new-day-has-come-for-its-long -suffering-neighbors/.

26 Foner, *Gateway to Freedom*, 151–52.

27 Kate E. R. Pickard, *The Kidnapped and the Ransomed. Being the Personal Recollections of Peter Still and His Wife "Vina," After Forty Years Of Slavery*, (Syracuse, N.Y.: William T. Hamilton, 1856), 249, https://docsouth.unc.edu /neh/pickard/pickard.html.

28 Fergus M. Bordewich, *Bound for Canaan: The Epic Story of the Underground Railroad, America's First Civil Rights Movement* (New York: Amistad Books, 2005), 357–61.

29 Bradford, *Scenes*, 20.

30 Still, *The Underground Rail Road*, 297.

31 Valerie Still, *Playing Black and Blue: Still I Rise,* (Palmyra, N.J.: Still Publications), 49.

32 Sarah Holder, "The City That Remade Its Police Department," *Bloomberg Businessweek*, June 4, 2020, https://www.bloomberg.com/news/articles /2020-06-04/how-camden-new-jersey-reformed-its-police-department.

33 Kevin Riordan, "Lawnside Mourns a Titan of the Community," *Philadelphia Inquirer*, May 10, 2012, https://www.inquirer.com/philly/columnists/kevin _riordan/20120510_Lawnside_mourns_a_titan_of_the_community.html.

34 Still, *The Underground Rail Road*, 5.

35 National Park Service, "Abolition," Statue of Liberty National Monument, retrieved June 2, 2020. https://www.nps.gov/stli/learn/historyculture /abolition.htm. See also Edward Berenson, *The Statue of Liberty: A Transatlantic Story*, (New Haven, Conn.: Yale University Press).

36 Ken Burns, "Our Monuments Are Representations of Myth, Not Fact," *Washington Post*, June 23, 2020, https://www.washingtonpost.com/opinions /2020/06/23/ken-burns-our-monuments-are-representations-myth-not-fact/.

37 Foner, *Gateway to Freedom*, 191.

38 Larson, *Bound for the Promised Land*, 137–38; Bradford, *Scenes*, 109–110.

39 Charles Dickens, *American Notes for General Circulation*, 1842.

40 Linda Wheeler, "The New York Draft Riots of 1863," *Washington Post*, April 29, 2013, https://www.washingtonpost.com/lifestyle/style/the-new-york-draft-riots-of-1863/2013/04/26/a1aacf52-a620-11e2-a8e2-5b98cb59187f_story.html.

41 Frederick Douglass, *Narrative of the Life of Frederick Douglass, an American Slave,* (Boston: Anti-Slavery Office, 1845), 107–108, https://docsouth.unc.edu/neh/douglass/douglass.html.

42 Foner, *Gateway to Freedom*, 44–45, 219.

43 Underground Railroad Education Center, Albany, N.Y., https://undergroundrailroadhistory.org/residence/.

44 Letter, Harriet Myers to William Jay, August 20, 1860, on display at Stephen and Harriet Myers House.

45 Foner, *Gateway to Freedom*, 29, 35–36; an account of Washington's negotiations with the British on the departure from New York is in the National Archives at https://founders.archives.gov/documents/Washington/99-01-02-11217.

46 Lisa Anderson, "Schuyler Flatts Burial Ground," New York State Museum, retrieved July 3, 2020, http://www.nysm.nysed.gov/research-collections/archaeology/bioarchaeology/research/schuyler-flatts-burial-ground.

47 Paul Grondahl, "14 Schuyler Flatts Slaves to Be Reburied in Albany Area," *Albany Times-Union*, June 17, 2016, https://www.timesunion.com/local/article/14-Schuyler-Flatts-slaves-to-be-reburied-in-8310456.php.

48 The original narrative of the Nalle rescue comes from Bradford, *Scenes in the Life of Harriet Tubman*, 88–89. The full story of the rescue and its aftermath is described in Scott Christianson, *Freeing Charles: The Struggle to Free a Slave on the Eve of the Civil War* (Urbana: University of Illinois Press, 2010).

49 Christianson, *Freeing Charles*, 200.

50 American Battlefield Trust, "Virginia Preservation Organizations and Civil War Trust Save Unique Civil War Site in Culpeper County," March 1, 2018, https://www.battlefields.org/news/virginia-preservation-organizations-and-civil-war-trust-save-unique-civil-war-site-culpeper.

51 Virginia Department of Historic Resources, "023-0068 Hansborough Ridge Winter Encampment District," updated June 6, 2022, https://www.dhr.virginia.gov/historic-registers/023-0068/.

52 Norman K. Dann, *Practical Dreamer: Gerrit Smith and the Crusade for Social Reform* (Hamilton, N.Y.: Log Cabin Books, 2009), 98.

53 Dann, *Practical Dreamer*, 447.

54 Dann, *Practical Dreamer*, xiii.

55 Ezra Klein Show interview, 2021, https://www.nytimes.com/2021/07/30 /podcasts/transcript-ezra-klein-interviews-ta-nehisi-coates-and-nikole -hannah-jones.html.

56 Josephine Pacheco, *The Pearl: A Failed Slave Escape on the Potomac*, (Chapel Hill: University of North Carolina Press, 2005), 120–122.

57 Pacheco, *The Pearl*, 241.

58 Alexandria, Virginia, historical marker at the site of the Edmonson Sisters Sculpture.

59 Bordewich, *Bound for Canaan*, 317; Dann, *Practical Dreamer*, 18; historical marker at Jesup Blair Park, Silver Spring, Md.

60 Dann, *Practical Dreamer*, 502.

61 Larson, *Bound for the Promised Land*, 189.

62 Dann, *Practical Dreamer*, 476.

63 Dann, *Practical Dreamer*, 489.

64 "Syracuse and the Underground Railroad," exhibition of the Special Collections Research Center, Syracuse University Library, September 30, 2005, https://library.syr.edu/digital/exhibits/u/undergroundrr/.

65 Daniel Webster, "Mr. Webster's Speeches at Buffalo, Syracuse, and Albany, May 1851," (New York: George Nesbitt and Co., 1851), 36, archived at Library of Congress and at https://archive.org/details/mrwebstersspeech 01web/page/n9/mode/2up.

66 Blight, *Frederick Douglass*, 234.

67 Bordewich, *Bound for Canaan*, 333.

68 "Frederick Douglass' Descendants Deliver His 'Fourth Of July' Speech," July 3, 2020, National Public Radio, https://www.npr.org/2020/07/03/884832594 /video-frederick-douglass-descendants-read-his-fourth-of-july-speech.

69 Bright, *Frederick Douglass*, 750, 754.

70 Bradford, *Scenes*, 27.

71 Jake Halpern, "The Underground Railroad for Refugees," *New Yorker*, March 13, 2017, https://www.newyorker.com/magazine/2017/03/13/the -underground-railroad-for-refugees.

72 Halpern, "The Underground Railroad for Refugees."

73 Ian Austen, "In Shift, Trudeau Says Canada Will Return Asylum Seekers to U.S.," *New York Times*, March 20, 2020, https://www.nytimes.com/2020/03/20 /world/canada/trudeau-asylum-seekers-coronavirus.html.

74 Michael Levenson, "4 Dead in Brutal Cold at U.S. Border Are Believed to Be Human Smuggling Victims," *New York Times*, January 20, 2022, https://www .nytimes.com/2022/01/20/us/four-dead-canada-us-border.html.

75 Larson, *Bound for the Promised Land*, 133–36.

76 Bradford, *Scenes*, 33.

77 J. Evans, "Abduction of a Slave," *New Orleans Times-Picayune*, August 4, 1841, 2, displayed at the Niagara Falls Underground Railroad Heritage Center.

78 Public Broadcasting Service, *The African Americans: Many Rivers to Cross*, episode 2, "The Age of Slavery," aired October 29, 2013, available at pbs.org.

79 Larson, *Bound for the Promised Land*, 12.

80 Toni Morrison, *Beloved*, (New York: Vintage Books, 1987), 16.

81 Bradford, *Scenes*, 7.

3. FREEDOM ROAD WEST

1 Imani Perry, *South to America*, (New York: HarperCollins, 2022), 324, 341.

2 Edward Baptist, *The Half Has Never Been Told: Slavery and the Making of American Capitalism*, (New York: Basic Books, 2014), 28.

3 Henry Louis Gates Jr., "What Was the Second Middle Passage?" *The African Americans: Many Rivers to Cross*, PBS, 2013, https://www.pbs.org/wnet /african-americans-many-rivers-to-cross/history/what-was-the-2nd-middle -passage/.

4 Albert Thrasher, *On to New Orleans: Louisiana's Heroic 1811 Slave Revolt*, (New Orleans: Cypress Press, 1998), 48.

5 Smith, *How the Word Is Passed*, 54.

6 Baptist, *The Half Has Never Been Told*, 58.

7 Leon Waters, personal communication, November 20, 2017.

8 Clint Smith, "The Young Black Activists Targeting New Orleans' Confederate Monuments," *New Republic*, May 18, 2017.

9 Ken Burns, "Our Monuments."

10 Mitchell Landrieu, "Truth: Remarks on the Removal of Confederate Monuments in New Orleans," Gallier Hall, City of New Orleans, May 19, 2017, https://www.nytimes.com/2017/05/23/opinion/mitch-landrieus-speech -transcript.html.

11 Thrasher, *On to New Orleans*, 118.

12 Perry, *South to America*, 344.

13 Baptist, *The Half Has Never Been Told*, 62.

14 A detailed accounting of what we know of the people in the revolt is at https://www.the1811slaverevolt.com.

15 *Women of Cancer Alley*, (Center for Constitutional Rights and Louisiana Bucket Brigade, 2018), documentary, https://ccrjustice.org/cancer-alley.

16 Smith, *How the Word is Passed*, 58.

17 Antonia Juhasz, "Louisiana's 'Cancer Alley' Is Getting Even More Toxic—But Residents Are Fighting Back," *Rolling Stone*, October 30, 2019, https://www.rollingstone.com/politics/politics-features/louisiana-cancer-alley-getting-more-toxic-905534/.

18 Victor Blackwell, Wayne Drash, and Christopher Lett, "Toxic Tensions in the Heart of 'Cancer Alley'," CNN, October 20, 2017, https://www.cnn.com/2017/10/20/health/louisiana-toxic-town/index.html.

19 Ruhan Nagra, Robert Taylor, Mary Hampton, and Lance Hilderbrand, "'Waiting to Die': Toxic Emissions and Disease Near the Denka Performance Elastomer Neoprene Facility in Louisiana's Cancer Alley," *Environmental Justice* 14, no. 1 (February 18, 2021), https://doi.org/10.1089/env.2020.0056.

20 Nina Lakhani, "Cancer Alley Campaigner Wins Goldman Prize for Environmental Defenders," *The Guardian* (US edition), June 15, 2021, https://www.theguardian.com/us-news/2021/jun/15/sharon-lavigne-goldman-prize-cancer-alley-campaigner.

21 Tristan Baurick, "'It's a Slam upon Our State': Sen. Bill Cassidy Rebukes Joe Biden over 'Cancer Alley' Remarks," *New Orleans Times-Picayune*, February 3, 2021, https://www.nola.com/news/environment/article_98b5dd56-665c-11eb-993d-ab9537e3b12f.html.

22 Lisa Friedman, "In 'Cancer Alley,' Judge Blocks Huge Petrochemical Plant," *New York Times*, September 15, 2022, https://www.nytimes.com/2022/09/15/climate/louisiana-judge-blocks-formosa-plant.html?action=click&module=Well&pgtype=Homepage&section=Climate%20and%20Environment.

23 Perry, *South to America*, 325.

24 Ted Gioia, *Delta Blues: The Life and Times of the Mississippi Masters Who Revolutionized American Music,* (New York: Norton, 2008), 46.

25 Gioia, *Delta Blues*, 87.

26 Douglas Blackmon, *Slavery by Another Name,* (New York: Doubleday, 2008), 7.

27 David Nakamura, "Justice Dept. Says Mississippi Allowed Unsafe State Prison Conditions," *Washington Post*, April 20, 2022, https://www.washingtonpost.com/national-security/2022/04/20/mississippi-prison-justice-parchman/.

28 Perry, *South to America*, 221.

29 Alan Lomax, *The Land Where the Blues Began,* (New York: New Press, 1993), 27.

30 Timothy Tyson, *The Blood of Emmett Till,* (New York: Simon and Schuster, 2017), 15.

31 PBS, *American Epic: Out of the Many, One*, 2017, transcript at https://www.pbs.org/wnet/american-epic/video/episode-103-many-one/.

32 PBS, *Out of the Many, One*.

33 Philip Ratcliffe, *Mississippi John Hurt: His Life, His Times, His Blues,* (Jackson: University Press of Mississippi, 2011), 70.

34 Ratcliffe, *Mississippi John Hurt*, 99.

35 Ratcliffe, *Mississippi John Hurt*, 128.

36 Public Broadcasting Service, *The African Americans: Many Rivers to Cross,* episode 2, "The Age of Slavery," aired October 29, 2013, available at pbs.org.

37 B. Brian Foster, "Antebellum Houses of the American South: What Happens Now?" *Veranda*, July/August 2021, https://www.veranda.com/decorating -ideas/a36422167/antebellum-houses/.

38 Jim Barnett and H. Clark Burkett, "The Forks in the Road Slave Market at Natchez," *Journal of Mississippi History*, 63, No. 3 (Fall 2001), https://www .mshistorynow.mdah.ms.gov/issue/the-forks-of-the-road-slave-market -at-natchez.

39 Greg Grandin, *The End of the Myth: From the Frontier to the Border Wall in the Mind of America,* (New York: Metropolitan Books, 2019), 51–52.

40 Winston Groom, *Shiloh 1862,* (Washington: National Geographic Society, 2012).

41 Donald L. Miller, *Vicksburg: Grant's Campaign That Broke the Confederacy,* (New York: Simon and Schuster, 2019), 335.

42 Groom, *Shiloh 1862*.

43 Ambrose Bierce, "What I Saw of Shiloh," in *The Ambrose Bierce Project*, ed. Craig E. Warren (Penn State University), https://courses.lumenlearning.com /suny-jcc-ushistory1os/chapter/primary-source-ambrose-bierce-recalls-his -experience-at-the-battle-of-shiloh-1881/.

44 C. F. Flood, *Grant's Final Victory: Ulysses S. Grant's Heroic Last Year,* (Philadelphia: De Capo Press, 2011).

45 Ron Chernow, *Grant,* (New York: Penguin Books, 2017), 928–54.

46 Chernow, *Grant*, 280.

47 Linda Barnickel, *Milliken's Bend: A Civil War Battle in History and Memory,* (Baton Rouge: Louisiana State University Press, 2013), 59–61.

48 Frederick Douglass, "Address for the Promotion of Colored Enlistments," speech in Philadelphia, July 6, 1863, in Blight, *Frederick Douglass*, 395.

49 Barnickel, *Milliken's Bend*, 2.

50 Ta-Nehisi Coates in *Grant*, episode 2, "Mr. Lincoln's General," May 26, 2020, The History Channel.

51 Barnickel, *Milliken's Bend*, 17.

52 William A. Dobak, *Freedom by the Sword: The U.S. Colored Troops, 1862–1867,* (New York: Skyhorse Publishing, 2013), 182.

53 Barnickel, *Milliken's Bend*, 90.

54 Barnickel, *Milliken's Bend*, 98.

55 Chernow, *Grant*, 283.

56 Chernow, *Grant*, 283.

57 Linda Barnickel, "Outrages and Murders, Louisiana, 1868," blog post, 2017, *Milliken's Bend*, https://millikensbend.com/blog/page/4/.

58 Charles Lane, "Not Far from Tulsa, a Quieter but Consequential Correction of the Historical Record," *Washington Post*, June 8, 2021, https://www .washingtonpost.com/opinions/2021/06/08/not-far-tulsa-quieter -consequential-correction-historical-record/. A marker at the site stated, "On this site occurred the Colfax Riot in which three white men and 150 negroes were slain. This event on April 13, 1873, marked the end of carpetbag misrule in the South." In May 2021, the marker was taken down.

59 Toni Morrison, "The Site of Memory" in *Inventing the Truth: The Art and Craft of Memoir*, 2nd ed., William Zinsser, ed. (Boston: Houghton Mifflin, 1995), 83–102, https://blogs.umass.edu/brusert/files/2013/03/Morrison _Site-of-Memory.pdf.

60 Jack Hurst, *Nathan Bedford Forrest: A Biography*, (New York: Alfred A. Knopf, 1993), 6.

61 Letter of Sgt. Achilles Clark, cited in John Cimprich, *Fort Pillow: A Civil War Massacre and Public Memory*, (Baton Rouge: Louisiana State University Press, 2005).

62 Cimprich, *Fort Pillow*, 129.

63 Cimprich, *Fort Pillow*, 94.

64 Cimprich, *Fort Pillow*, 82.

65 Eddy W. Davidson. *Nathan Bedford Forrest: In Search of the Enigma*, (New York: Pelican Publishing, 2007), 474.

66 Hurst, *Nathan Bedford Forrest*, 4.

67 Ryan Poe, "Memphis Removes Confederate Statues from Downtown Parks," *Memphis Commercial Appeal*, December 20, 2017, https://www.commercial appeal.com/story/news/government/city/2017/12/20/memphis-council-votes -immediately-remove-confederate-statues/960707001/; Johnny Diaz, "Bust of Klan Leader Removed From Tennessee State Capitol," *New York Times*, July 23, 2021, https://www.nytimes.com/2021/07/23/us/nathan-bedford -forrest-bust.html.

68 Steve Inskeep, *Jacksonland: President Andrew Jackson, Cherokee Chief John Ross, and a Great American Land Grab*, (New York: Penguin Press, 2015), 4.

69 Brian Hicks, "The Cherokees vs. Andrew Jackson," *Smithsonian*, March 1, 2011, https://www.smithsonianmag.com/history/the-cherokees-vs-andrew -jackson-277394/.

70 Inskeep, *Jacksonland*, 172.

71 Inskeep, *Jacksonland*, 87.

72 Grant Freeman, *Indian Removal: Emigration of the Five Civilized Tribes of Indians*, (Norman: University of Oklahoma Press, 1932), 306.

73 Cited in Freeman, *Indian Removal*, 308.

74 Russell Thornton, "Cherokee Population Losses During the Trail of Tears," *Ethnohistory* 3, no. 4 (1984): 289–300.

75 Diane Perrine Coon, 2006. "Underground Railroad Network to Freedom: The Story of Georgetown District in Madison, Indiana," Indiana Department of Natural Resources, 2006, https://www.in.gov/dnr/historic/files/georgetown.pdf.

76 National Park Service, "Underground Railroad Network to Freedom: Georgetown Neighborhood," accessed January 7, 2021, https://www.nps.gov/nr/travel/madison/Georgetown_Neighborhood.html.

77 Blaine Hudson and Anne Butler, interviewed in "Kentucky's Underground Railroad—Passage to Freedom: The Documentary," KET Public Broadcasting, 2000, https://education.ket.org/resources/kentuckys-underground-railroad-passage-freedom/.

78 Kentucky Historical Society Marker, 1996, "Slave Trading in Louisville." S. 2nd Street and W. Main Street, Louisville, Ky.

79 Fergus Bordewich, *Bound for Canaan*, 202–204.

80 John H. Tibbets, *Reminiscences of Slavery Times*, unpublished chronicle (Lancaster, Ind.: Eleutherian College, 1884), cited in Coon, "Underground Railroad Network."

81 Bordewich, *Bound for Canaan*, 205.

82 George DeBaptiste, *Encyclopedia of Detroit*, Detroit Historical Society, accessed January 13, 2021, https://detroithistorical.org/learn/encyclopedia-of-detroit/debaptiste-george.

83 "Kentucky's Underground Railroad—Passage to Freedom: The Documentary," KET Public Broadcasting, 2000, https://education.ket.org/resources/kentuckys-underground-railroad-passage-freedom/.

84 Bordewich, *Bound for Canaan*, 190.

85 John P. Parker, *His Promised Land: The Autobiography of John P. Parker, Former Slave and Conductor on the Underground Railroad*, ed. Stuart Sprague, (New York: W. W. Norton and Co., 1998), Kindle edition, location 1367.

86 Bordewich, *Bound for Canaan*, 371.

87 Parker, *His Promised Land*, location 134.

88 Parker, *His Promised Land*, location 1082.

89 Josiah Henson, *The Life of Josiah Henson, Formerly a Slave, Now an Inhabitant of Canada, as Narrated by Himself* (Boston: Arthur D. Phelps, 1849), 86, https://docsouth.unc.edu/neh/henson49/henson49.html.

90 Display panel, Josiah Henson Museum and Park, Rockville, Maryland.

91 Henson, *The Life of Josiah Henson*, 1.

92 Baptist, *The Half Has Never Been Told*, 497.

93 Jaimie Ferguson Kuhns, *Sharp Flashes of Lightning Come from Black Clouds: The Life of Josiah Henson* (Silver Spring: Maryland National Capital Park and Planning Commission), 69.

94 Henson, *The Life of Josiah Henson*, 23.

95 Henson, *The Life of Josiah Henson*, 50–51.

96 Josiah Henson, *Uncle Tom's Story of His Life*, (Boston: B. B. Russell and Co., 1879), 84, https://docsouth.unc.edu/neh/henson/henson.html.

97 Henson, *Uncle Tom's Story of His Life*, 90.

98 Helen Rappaport, *Queen Victoria: A Biographical Companion*, (Santa Barbara, Calif.: ABC-CLIO, 2003).

99 Display panel, Josiah Henson Museum and Park, Rockville, Md.

100 Benjamin Quarles, *Allies for Freedom: Blacks and John Brown*, (New York: Oxford University Press, 1974), 72.

101 Quarles, *Allies for Freedom*, 78.

102 "Lewis Sheridan Leary Shawl," description of museum collection item, Ohio History Connection, accessed June 28, 2022, https://ohiomemory.org/digital/collection/p267401coll32/id/20719.

103 Winston Groom, *Shiloh 1862*, 54–56.

104 Baptist, *The Half Has Never Been Told*, 393.

105 Langston Hughes, "October 16," 1931. Accessed at https://emergingcivilwar.com/2019/10/16/october-the-sixteenth-alive-with-ghosts-today/.

106 Thomas Cather, tourist, from display panel at Harpers Ferry National Historical Park, 1836.

107 "An Ordinary Shawl with an Extraordinary Story," blog post, February 20, 2014, Ohio History Connection, https://www.ohiohistory.org/an-ordinary-shawl-with-an-extraordinary-story/.

108 Steven Lubet and Rachel Maines, "This Shawl Belonged to Langston Hughes (True) and Was Worn by One of John Brown's Men at Harpers Ferry (Well . . .)," *Humanities* 37, no. 3 (Summer 2016), https://www.neh.gov/humanities/2016/summer/feature/shawl-belonged-langston-hughes-true-and-was-worn-one-john-brown's-men-harpers-ferry-well.

4. FREEDOM CITY

1 "Freedom City: Uncovering Toronto's Black History," 2015, Toronto Public Library, http://omeka.tplcs.ca/virtual-exhibits/exhibits/show/freedom-city/freedom-seekers.

2   Gareth Newfield, "The Coloured Corps: Black Canadians and the War of 1812," 2016, The Canadian Encyclopedia, accessed November 22, 2021, https://www.thecanadianencyclopedia.ca/en/article/the-coloured-corps-african-canadians-and-the-war-of-1812.

3   Display panel at Freedom House, Alexandria, Virginia; Hansi Lo Wang, "A New Life For An Old Slave Jail," November 19, 2013, National Public Radio, https://www.npr.org/sections/codeswitch/2013/11/19/245983186/a-new-life-for-an-old-slave-jail.

4   Edward Ball, "Retracing Slavery's Trail of Tears," *Smithsonian Magazine*, November 2015, https://www.smithsonianmag.com/history/slavery-trail-of-tears-180956968/.

5   Clint Smith, *How the Word Is Passed*, 289.

6   Full Text of the Texas Law Restricting Classroom Talk on Racism (HB 3979), Education Week, July 15, 2021, https://www.edweek.org/policy-politics/full-text-of-the-texas-law-restricting-classroom-talk-on-racism-hb-3979/2021/07.

7   *True Justice: Bryan Stevenson's Fight for Equality*, HBO documentary, 2019.

8   Jill Lepore, "When Black History is Unearthed, Who Gets to Speak for the Dead?" *The New Yorker*, October 4, 2021, https://www.newyorker.com/magazine/2021/10/04/when-black-history-is-unearthed-who-gets-to-speak-for-the-dead.